MW01199099

Praise fc
and *Iowa Ethiopia*

"Finished the book last night, with tears in my eyes. If I didn't know better, I would say this story has to be a tale of fiction, it's so remarkable."
—Lisa Boonstra Burg, Writer

"Oh my. *Sioux Center Sudan* is beautiful. Heartbreaking. Inspiring."
**—Rev. Dr. Travis Else, Campus Pastor
First Reformed Church, Sioux Center, Iowa**

"Moving, thought-provoking, and beautifully written. I loved this book."
—Kay Gillette, Teacher

"So accessible and real. I felt like I was living the story with Arlene and her family."
—Rev. Jonathan Opgenorth, President , Words of Hope Ministry

"Jeff Barker is a master storyteller who gets at the heart of God's call to mission."
—Joe Culumber, Pastor and Missionary

"I could not put it down and finished in two days."
—Nicole Wede, Instructor in Nursing, Northwestern College

"*Iowa Ethiopia: A Missionary Nurse's Journey Continues* was a captivating read that often surprised me. Those who wrestle with questions about the will of God and why evil often seems to prevail will find genuine personal insights from the fascinating episodes of a beloved missionary who lived her life on the edge. The book is a jewel."
**—Gerald Borchert, Author
*Christ and Chaos: Biblical Keys to Ethical Questions***

Zambia
HOME

Other Books by Jeff Barker

Sioux Center Sudan: A Missionary Nurse's Journey
First book in the Arlene Schuiteman Story

Iowa Ethiopia: A Missionary Nurse's Journey Continues
Second book in the Arlene Schuiteman Story

Performing the Plays of the Bible:
Seven Ancient Scripts and Our Journey to Return Them
to the Stage (coauthored with Thomas Boogaart)

The Storytelling Church:
Adventures in Reclaiming the Role of Story in Worship

Zambia
HOME

A MISSIONARY NURSE ENDURES

JEFF BARKER

HENDRICKSON
PUBLISHERS

Zambia Home: A Missionary Nurse Endures

© 2021 Jeff Barker

Published by Hendrickson Publishers
an imprint of Hendrickson Publishing Group
Hendrickson Publishers, LLC
P. O. Box 3473
Peabody, Massachusetts 01961-3473
www.hendricksonpublishinggroup.com

978-1-68307-308-6

Scripture quoted in this book, unless otherwise noted, are the author's own translations. On a few occasions, scriptures are recorded as they were paraphrased within historical documents.

Scripture quotations marked (TLB) are taken from The Living Bible, copyright © 1971. Used by permission of Tyndale House Publishers, Inc., Carol Stream, Illinois 60188. All rights reserved.

Scripture quotations marked (NLT) are taken from the Holy Bible, New Living Translation, copyright ©1996, 2004, 2007, 2013, 2015 by Tyndale House Foundation. Used by permission of Tyndale House Publishers, Inc., Carol Stream, Illinois 60188. All rights reserved.

Scripture quotations marked (NIV) are taken from the Holy Bible, New International Version®, NIV®. Copyright © 1973, 1978, 1984, 2011 by Biblica, Inc.™ Used by permission of Zondervan. All rights reserved worldwide. www.zondervan.com The "NIV" and "New International Version" are trademarks registered in the United States Patent and Trademark Office by Biblica, Inc.™

Scripture quotations marked (NRSV) are taken from New Revised Standard Version Bible, copyright © 1989 by the Division of Christian Education of the National Council of the Churches of Christ in the United States of America. Used by permission. All rights reserved.

Portions of the stories in this book were previously disseminated by the author in the plays *Zambia Home* and *Arlene: An African Trilogy*. Quotations from Arlene Schuiteman's unpublished diaries and collections of letters (her letters and others sent to her) have occasionally been edited for clarity, brevity, and fluidity. The originals will eventually be available to researchers at the Joint Archives of Holland in Holland, Michigan.

The prayer by Marie Ann Traver was first published in *Evangelical Visitor* (October 25, 1975), 8.

The Tonga proverbs are from Isaac Mumpande's collection shared at this site: http://www.mulonga.net/tonga-culture/262-tonga-proverbs-by-isaac-mumpande

Printed in the United States of America

First Printing — February 2021

Library of Congress Control Number: 2020952578

For Jackson,
storyteller, musician,
and gospel man

One generation shall laud your works to another,
and shall declare your mighty acts.

Psalm 145:4 (NRSV)

Insya nchenjezu njiichija kichebuuka.

A clever buck is one that runs forward
and looks back at the same time.

Tonga Proverb

 *Contents*

Acknowledgments		xiii
Prologue		xix
Map of Ethiopia		xxv
1	Wilderness	1
2	Labor	18
3	Home	23
4	Mail	25
5	Spirit	41
6	Time	49
7	Josh	55
8	Medicine	62
9	Chickens	66
10	Daughter	73
11	Matthew	76
12	Iteffa	100
13	Strangler	104
14	Resignation	114
15	Water	126

16   GRADUATION   134

17   CHIEF   145

18   DORIS   152

19   ANGELS   160

20   CHAPEL   169

21   HEADACHE   182

22   MOUNTAINTOP   192

SELECTED BIBLIOGRAPHY   205

PHOTOGRAPHS   207

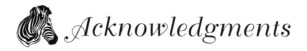 # Acknowledgments

Arlene's lifetime collection of journals and letters are the basis of this book as well as the two books and four plays that have preceded it. Beyond her own writing, Arlene has put countless hours into supporting the work of my students and me. Her patience, courage, intelligence, wit, and wisdom have been nothing short of a joy, enriching us beyond measure. Even though I am this book's writer, some of the best phrases come from Arlene's own words—words crafted in faithfulness at the end of her many exhausting days serving as a missionary nurse and educator. I do not know how she kept up her practice of journaling, but she did.

Arlene has been a diarist throughout her entire adult life. If she had not kept these records, the details of her experiences would have been forgotten before I met her. In addition to her journaling, Arlene has been a disciplined letter writer and a filer of old letters, both sent and received. These journals, letters, and other papers are a remarkable collection, a unique glimpse into the landscape of a soul. Arlene's sharing of these materials is a profound gift of trust.

Arlene's lifelong friend was Eleanor Vandevort, who I came to know as Vandy or Nyarial (the name given to her by the Nuer tribe). Others know her as Van. Vandy's book *A Leopard Tamed* is a treasure, a book written ahead of its time in 1968. It conveys an intelligent and gripping perspective on the Nuer culture of the South Sudan. By the time I met Vandy, her book was out of print; but thankfully, Hendrickson Publishers re-released *A Leopard Tamed* in 2018. Besides containing historic photos, the new volume includes an introduction by Elisabeth Elliot's daughter, Valerie Elliot Shepard.

Although Vandy has gone to be with the Lord, she would surely throw up her hands in delight to know that her dear friend Arlene's stories also continue to be shared. Vandy was an excellent editor and encourager to me during each of the plays I wrote about Arlene, plays presented in the United States, Japan, and Ethiopia (*Sioux Center Sudan, Iowa Ethiopia,* and *Zambia Home*). Next, I combined those plays into a lengthy (and slightly different) play called *Arlene: An African Trilogy,* which was presented at Northwestern College in Orange City, Iowa, as a celebratory culmination of a decade-long theatrical project. While the plays cover only a fraction of what you now read, the helpers of that foundational dramatic project should be remembered. These theatre artists were patient and courageous on the journeys of those three world-premiere productions: Kristen Olson-Jones Brind, Kristi Woodyard Christenson, Stephen Stonebraker, Margareta DeBoer Maxon, Lois Estell, Tessa Drijfhout-Rosier, Rachel Foulks, Megan Hodgin, Brady Greer Huffman, Matt Hulstein, Tracey Pronk Hulstein, Micah Trapp, Brett Vander Berg, Lindsay Westerkamp Bauer, Dan Laird, Hannah Barker Nickolay, Jackson Nickolay, Dan Sikkema, Aleah Stenberg, Kristin Trease, Loam Schuster, Amalia Vasquez, Huiyu Lin, Tesla McGillivray Kasten, Brianne Hassman Christiansen, Jacob Christiansen, Marisol Seys, Ali Sondreal Fernandez, Eric Van Der Linden, and Megan Weidner.

Actors in the original production of *Arlene: An Africa Trilogy* were John Amodeo, Christa Curl Baker, Brianne Hassman Christiansen, Jacob Christiansen, Megan Cole, Amanda Hays Duncan, Abby McCubbin, and Megan Vipond. The wonderful design team included Amber Beyer, Amber Huizenga, Theresa Larrabee, Jana Latchaw Milbourn, Jackson Nickolay, Jonathan Sabo, Drew Schmidt, Rachel Hanson Starkenburg, and Rowan Sullivan. Alex Wendel, Tiffany White-Hach, and Logan Wright supported Karen Bohm Barker at the director's table.

Isaac Mumpande's Tonga proverbs collection was helpful for the play as well as this book. Doug Norris was helpful in sharing his personal experiences of Zambia, and his excellent photographs can be viewed at https://dougnorris.zenfolio.com.

Dr. David Byer, who first connected Arlene with Zambia, provided seed funds for a research trip to Macha. Arlene agreed to go even though she was eighty-seven at the time! We used that trip to visit not only Zambia, but to make arrangements in Ethiopia for performances of the second play in the trilogy. During our time in Zambia, many of Arlene's old friends met with us and provided assistance. There are too many to mention them all, but of greatest help was Dr. Phil Thuma. He arranged our entire schedule while in Macha. Other gracious hosts included Dr. John Spurrier, Enoch and Lastinah Shamapani, and Abraham M'Hango (the acting hospital administrator) and his wife Vera (who is, like Arlene, a nurse). Doreen Sitali, the head tutor at Macha Nurses Training School, welcomed us into her office, where Arlene herself used to sit behind the desk.

Matthew Tura Gichile is the founding president of New Generation University College in Ethiopia. Matthew first met Arlene in Zambia, so he shows up in this book. He graciously provided details for his side of the story. He first showed up in my life when he suggested that we perform the play *Iowa Ethiopia* in Addis Ababa, and he helped make that happen.

Esther Spurrier provided recorded music and language help. Dwight Thomas gave helpful counsel. Northwestern College Theatre Office Manager Becky Donahue was crucial in the early phases of this third book, along with student assistant Karisa Meier. Colleen Van Berkum cheerfully helped me with resources about the history of Sioux Center. Avonell Rutherford amazingly collected and passed along to me nearly fifty years of letters from Arlene.

Joonna Trapp, expert teacher of creative nonfiction, provided inspiring and supportive counsel in the earliest phases of the book portion of this project. I could not have a better friend and cheerleader than Joonna, and I have kept her notes posted on my wall to read whenever I felt I had lost my literary way.

I offer special thanks to other early readers: Grada Kiel, Adel Aiken, Roxanne Netzler, and Joanne Barker. My sisters, Chris

Jackson and Jane Carpenter, have cheered their brother on in remarkable ways.

Doug Calsbeek of the *Sioux County Capital Democrat* facilitated a prepublication serialization of portions of the books and gave valuable editing advice throughout the journey of serialization. I am grateful to Katherine Lempares, who created the artistic renderings of Zambia and the African continent. Vaughn Donahue, a fine graphic artist, has helped in more ways than I can count.

Carrie Martin and Patricia Anders of Hendrickson Publishers have been amazing encouragers. Patricia's attention to the editing details has been nothing short of remarkable. Meg Rusick, Hendrickson's marketing director, Lynnette Pennings of Rose Publishing, and typesetter Phil Frank have been champions for helping a little-known story attract the attention it needs. Artist-in-residence Drew McCall created an original zebra image for this book; the zebra is an important animal to Zambia and is featured on the Zambian Coat of Arms.

Kim Van Es is the gracious, good-humored, and wise content editor of early drafts, whose creative and razor-sharp way with words is present in every paragraph. I consider her friendship to the project a true godsend. Her husband, Dr. Jerry Van Es, proved to be an added blessing by providing valuable medical perspective on countless occasions.

Other immediate family members have lavished their encouragement upon me. My wife and colleague Karen has been the project's detailed and faithful literary coach. She is the one who heard every first "Listen to this!" and "Here's another chapter." She is a fine writer, teacher, artist, and critic, and I trust her feedback more than anyone else. My son Daniel is a fine writer and podcaster, and I have always appreciated his thoughtful and honest feedback. My composer son Joseph has written music for and consulted on several of these projects. My daughter-in-law Kay could be counted on to quickly read pages and provide insightful feedback throughout the process. My son-in-law Jackson, to whom this book is dedicated, is a creative and patient theatre artist, and it was a joy to watch him fall in love with my daughter Hannah as they worked on two of the Arlene plays.

Speaking of Hannah, she poured her heart into enacting Arlene. Eventually, Hannah became the archivist of Arlene's slide collection, working with Arlene along with my colleague Drew Schmidt to create descriptions and post the collection online. That collection may be found at http://portfolios.nwciowa.edu/arlene/default2.aspx. Hannah loves language and always nudges her father to be a better writer. She is amazing to me. I wish I were half the poet she is. There have been many more friends on this storytelling journey. They know who they are, and I hope they will forgive me for not mentioning each and every one of them by name.

I must end with a final thank you to Arlene. As I write these words, she is nearing her ninety-seventh birthday. The world remains in the throes of a pandemic that has made Arlene's world smaller than it has ever been. She still has a sharp mind and excellent health; but because of the virus, she has not been able to attend her church for months and currently is not even allowed to walk the hallways of her apartment complex. She and I can talk on the phone, however, and she receives the mail I leave at the entrance of her building. In these ways, she has participated every step of the way in the telling of this story—a precious gift she has given to me and to you.

Jeff Barker
Orange City, Iowa

 *Prologue*

Morning on the farm started early and noisily. Sleeping in was impossible. There were horses to feed, cows to milk, and eggs to gather. The eight-member crew of the compact, two-story house burst into rhythm, clattering up and down the steep stairs and bustling in and out of the narrow kitchen whose long table filled the room.

Harriet, Arlene, and Bernice—the three eldest of the six Schuiteman daughters—taught in the country schools north of Sioux Center. The next daughter, Grada, was catching the bus into town for high school. The two youngest, Joyce and Milly, were attending Welcome Number Four, the one-room school where their Pa had gone to school and where Arlene was now the instructor. These were the late 1940s—that sliver of in-between years for the Schuiteman sisters immediately following World War II, before any of the sisters were married, and before Arlene received the miraculous calling that would lead her into a thirty-four-year missionary career on the African continent. At age twenty-four, Arlene was writing in the *Five Year Diary* (her second one) that she had received for her birthday on January 3, 1948. Each night, she prepared her next day's lesson plans and then summarized the day past with a few lines in her journal before drifting off to sleep in the upstairs of the house her grandfather built, the only home Arlene had ever known.

After chores, breakfast, family devotions, clean-up, and good-byes, Arlene served as chauffeur of the Model A Ford, dropping Harriet and Bernice off at their school, one of the few two-room schools in the county. Joyce and Milly did not ride in with their three older sisters since teachers went early. The ruts carved in the dirt road kept Arlene on course until she arrived at her own little square school building. Pulling up close, she turned off the engine and experienced her first silence of the morning.

She then gathered her books, papers, and lunch bucket out of the back of the car and temporarily deposited them on the bench inside the school door. Tugging off her overshoes and coat, she arranged them neatly in the hallway as a model for her students to observe. During the winter months, she started a coal fire so the schoolhouse would be warm when the students stomped in from the neighboring farms. She strode along the wall of windows and turned at the recitation bench, where later in the day she would call the students up, grade by grade, for lessons and discussion. Arriving behind her desk in front of the long blackboard, she knew the stillness wouldn't last much longer, and she quickly settled into her round-backed wooden chair. Plenty of natural light flooded the room. Until the students arrived, it was "quiet time." She reached for her Bible.

The spiritual disciplines of her earlier life had tended to be corporate: Sunday worship, post-mealtime Bible reading, and family prayers. In her early adult years, Arlene came to understand that solitude and silence had to be created. The effort was worthwhile, however, because it empowered her own Bible study and contemplative prayer. From nineteen years of age onward, she engaged in the personal practice of setting aside a specific time every day to focus on things of the Spirit.

The habits Arlene nurtured in her twenties strengthened and matured throughout the following decades. Eventually, her spiritual practices included tithing, fasting, simplicity, confession, and what she came to call her "temple exercises." These latter activities alluded to the apostle Paul's reminder that one's body is the temple of the Holy Spirit (1 Corinthians 6:19). As a medical professional, Arlene understood the importance of maintaining her body. As a

Christ-follower, she understood that physical upkeep was related to her faith; she was not her own—she had been purchased by the blood of Jesus for the glory of God (1 Corinthians 6:20).

Years later, she would come to call her early morning refuge, "My time with Jesus." But she knew better than to think that her life could be divided into distinct areas of the spiritual, physical, emotional, social, and so on. Her whole life was lived with Jesus, including all the practices she considered precious to her well-being: work, play, planning, cleaning, fellowship, singing, the arts, reading, and writing—always writing. She had no idea what her writing would become. She started her journaling because her grandmother had commended it. When she landed on the mission field in the South Sudan of 1955, her writing was both therapy and a memory aid, helping her, like missionaries of Bible times, to write the letters necessary to stay connected to her supporters across the world. Eventually, her journaling became part of her spiritual discipline, including written prayers and personal prophecies. She always held her journals close. They were private, not intended for public consumption. But those very journals would one day become the basis of plays and books, including this one.

Beyond her daily journaling and almost daily letter writing, she wrote highlights for each month as part of her written summary of every year. She often listed the books she read and the plays she saw. Her favorite books included missionary biographies as well as the works of C. S. Lewis and George MacDonald. She saw Shakespeare plays whenever she could and attended classical concerts, which were popular in Africa since they cut across language barriers.

In 1977, Arlene's list of reflections included sins. This started when she spent a couple of weeks in Germany (on her way home from her second field of service in Ethiopia) at Canaan, a retreat center operated by the Evangelical Sisters of Mary. There, through the writings of Basilea Schlink, one of the leaders at Canaan who wrote about the joy of regularly confessing sin, Arlene was reminded of the gift of repentance. As with many Christians throughout the centuries, Arlene struggled with an existential tension between her yearning for sanctification and the certainty of her fallen nature. She believed with the ancient prophet Isaiah that even her righteous deeds were like filthy rags (Isaiah 64:6). During her time at Canaan, Arlene took out a piece of flimsy, gray stationary and (using her blue fine-point pen and tiny printing) catalogued her sins, crafting what she called a "mirror for her conscience." Most of the sins she listed were nonspecific, but she was nevertheless hard on herself. She acknowledged her perfectionism and a tendency toward pride and worrying about what others thought of her, confessing, "I want to look better than I am." She also confessed self-reliance, too many possessions, and a certain callousness toward the poverty she encountered every day on the streets of Addis Ababa. She was demanding honesty of herself.

As she wrote out this list, a particular memory arose. Like all medical professionals, she had faced difficult ethical decisions, often made in times of extreme duress. One day she found herself as the attending nurse while a doctor performed an abortion. The event had never made it into her journals, and even now there were few specifics. But it was a memory that would not go away, and she wrote it down, adding, "Memories need healing."

She also included on her list of confessions that she wanted to be married. One of her lengthy struggles was between her desire to be wholly satisfied with God and her wish to have a mate. She regretted that wish for a spouse, sometimes denigrating it as lust, but there it was. That longing rarely appears in her journals, but it was a thorn in her flesh.

Arlene's annual written summaries included songs and Bible passages. She especially loved hymns—such as "Jesus Paid It All," "It is Well with My Soul," and "Great Is Thy Faithfulness"—and she cited Scripture verses that were special guides to her:

Be still before the LORD and wait patiently for him.
(Psalm 37:7a)

Do not be discouraged, for the LORD your God will be with you wherever you go. (Joshua 1:9b)

My grace is sufficient for you, for my strength is made perfect in weakness. (2 Corinthians 12:9)

For to me to live is Christ, and to die is gain.
(Philippians 1:21 KJV)

One of her favorite verses was a translation she found of Proverbs 4:12a: "As you go, your way shall be opened up step by step before you."

Arlene was a planner, so she needed reminders that much of life must be lived one step at a time: she could not cross a bridge until she came to it. Such was her understanding of faith, of following God, that the prophet Habakkuk held particular guidance for her:

Though the fig tree does not bud and there are no grapes on the vines, though the olive crop fails and the fields produce no food, though there are no sheep in the pen and no cattle in the stalls, yet I will rejoice in the LORD, I will be joyful in God my Savior. The Sovereign LORD is my strength. He makes my feet like the feet of a deer. He enables me to tread on the heights.
(Habakkuk 3:17–19 NIV)

In reflecting on this passage, Arlene wrote the following:

Habakkuk thanks God in advance for the deliverance he does not see. This is faith. God tells us to trust Him because we know what He has done in the past. We know Him personally because He revealed Himself to us. We know about Him because His ways are recorded in the Bible.

Though Arlene had scaled spiritual heights in Ethiopia, her Shepherd had not selected her to stay on the green mountains of that ancient land. She would now be called down to the dry and hot plateaus of the southeastern African bush, to a new culture, and to the dangers of malaria and war. There, in Zambia, she would also encounter a mysterious and deadly new disease that would soon spread throughout the world.

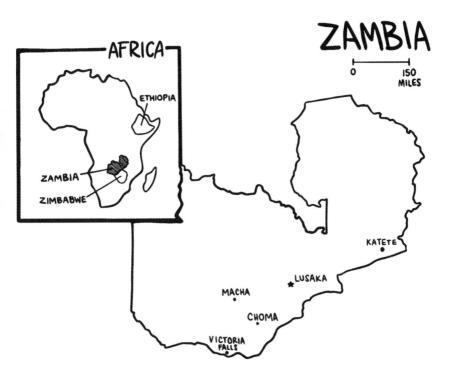

1

Wilderness

Chuungwe wuluka chamana nchwakkalilide.
Crow, fly away because what you came for is done.

Up early and Sister Mechthild came with a candle and sang a farewell song for me. Brother Immanuel took me to Frankfurt. Did not have to pay excess baggage, so sent the German Marks back to the Evangelical Sisterhood of Mary.

February 17, 1977

Boarding an early-morning flight out of Frankfurt for Logan Airport in Boston, Massachusetts, Arlene Schuiteman settled next to a woman about her own age. Frieda, now from Indiana, was born in Germany in the 1920s and had just returned to her homeland for her mother's funeral. Through the long hours of the transatlantic flight, the women swapped stories.

Arlene summarized her two decades as a Christian missionary on the African continent. She described her eight years of nursing in the Sudan at the Nasir clinic and hospital, which locals called "the place of magic." She told of the pride of tribal markings cut into faces, the trading of cattle for wives, and the river's rule over travel with its annual rise and fall. She talked of the seemingly endless civil war.

Arlene went on to share of her recently completed eleven years of teaching "dressers" ("one who dresses wounds"), which is another term for "nurses" in Ethiopia. She recounted the spiritual revival in the western mountains with its healings, exorcisms, and passionate worship. She depicted her final year in the capital city of Addis Ababa with its nightly gunfire and bodies on the streets at sunrise. In both countries, the government had forced her to leave, very much against her will.

Frieda soon opened the book of her own journey. During the Second World War, when she was a young mother, she had been arrested by the Nazis while her husband managed to escape. Perhaps she was Jewish, but she did not disclose to Arlene the reason for her arrest. The Nazis transported Frieda and her four-month-old to a concentration camp. When they arrived at the camp, the baby was wrenched from Frieda's arms, and she watched in horror as a soldier swung the child against a wall, crushing her baby's head.

Frieda somehow survived the grief of loss and the deprivation of prison life. But her husband assumed the worst and remarried before Frieda was set free after the war. She moved to England and fell in love with a surgeon. Together, they emigrated to Indianapolis to start life anew. For some reason, her husband's medical credentials would not transfer, so he started a business of building wooden cabinets. They had three children and life was good, until her second husband was diagnosed with cancer and was taken quite suddenly. Frieda despaired and thought she might kill herself. Then, while listening to a radio program, she gave her heart to Jesus.

Arlene believed in miracles, so Frieda's account did not surprise her. She believed that the Spirit of God worked through things such as radio programs and airplane seat assignments. Arlene's conversation with Frieda reminded her of what Jesus had said: "In the world you will have trouble. But take heart! I have overcome the world" (John 16:33 NIV).

Landing in Boston, the women prayed, embraced, and said goodbye. Arlene wrote Frieda's story in her journal that night, knowing she would need reminders of grace in the year to come. Although she did not expect this to be an easy year, she understood the necessity of going home. It was now more than four years since she had set foot stateside, let alone her hometown.

On her second morning back in Sioux Center, Iowa, on March 2, 1977, Arlene's alarm clock failed to ring. When she awoke at 6:15 in the predawn dark, her brother-in-law Henry was already waiting in the driveway. For the John G. Schuiteman family, tardiness was inexcusable, and Arlene flung herself out the door in a matter of minutes.

There was some question as to whether or not they should be traveling that day. Snow was forecast, but Arlene's trunks had arrived in Omaha, and she did not want them left sitting outside on the receiving dock. Those boxes contained the last vestiges of her life in Ethiopia and were therefore precious to her.

The sun rose during their three-hour trek southward. They had no trouble finding the receiving dock, and the collection charge was only two dollars and fifty cents. As they turned north toward home, the snow began to fall. Henry soon drove slower and slower.

"Do you think we should stop?" Arlene wondered aloud.

"Maybe," said her white-knuckled brother-in-law, but he drove on.

They made it to Sioux City, where Arlene had graduated from nursing school twenty-three years earlier. They crawled forward into the storm. While passing through Le Mars, about halfway between Sioux City and Sioux Center, the truck began to sputter. Since they had only a few more miles to go, Henry ignored the truck's groanings, bucking the snowdrifts all the way to the southern edge of Sioux Center. When the blowing snow finally killed the engine, Arlene and Henry got out and slogged into Holland House to borrow the use of the restaurant's phone to call for a tow from Mouw Motors. Although they were less than a mile from Arlene's home, it was blowing too hard to walk even that short distance.

The tow truck arrived, and the weary travelers climbed into the cab with the driver. He delivered Arlene back to her family home, the brick house on Second Avenue. After a struggle to clear the ice and snow enough to open the garage door, they moved Arlene's precious freight inside.

That exhausting, challenging day portended the year to come.

The official name of the year for Arlene was "furlough." The intention of a furlough is always relationships. It is an opportunity for missionaries to reestablish connection with their home culture and supporting churches. It is a time to rebuild the bonds that would sustain a return to fruitful ministry. A furloughing missionary rejoins their extended family, their sending church, and other churches of their home denomination. A furlough requires "deputation," which—before the days of social media—demanded extensive travel, giving speeches and slide presentations, while encouraging congregations to support the mission program of their denomination through prayers and financial contributions. At least, Arlene did not feel personally responsible for the raising of funds, and for that she was deeply grateful. This was a distinction between being sent by a denomination as opposed to an independent missionary organization that required its people to secure a set level of financial commitment prior to embarking for the field.

Arlene felt her only responsibility was to tell her story. Nevertheless, deputation was not Arlene's favorite activity. This nurse educator was comfortable alongside a hospital bed or lecturing in a classroom, but she dreaded formal speechmaking and crowded fellowship halls. Those activities tended to drain her. Her supervisor, Glenn Bruggers of the Reformed Church in America, knew Arlene well enough to urge her to take time for recuperation before she set out on this grueling tour.

As important as both rest and deputation were, there was one equally important task of this furlough year: Arlene, along with her denomination's mission board, would need to determine her next mission assignment. This decision would take practical calculations as well as spiritual discernment. Obviously, they would all seek God's will in the matter. South Sudan and Ethiopia were obvious candidates since she was familiar with those languages and cultures, but her safety in those countries was questionable. As much as Arlene might wish to return to her two previous homes on the African continent, they were dubious options unless there were major governmental shifts. There would be time to process it, Glenn assured her. What was important now was for her to rest prior to her preparation for the other duties of furlough. Arlene readily agreed. She needed time. This furlough was long overdue. Unfortunately, its onset had been relatively sudden—driven by violent and inscrutable political changes. Arlene had been torn away from her friends and ministry, which left her in an ongoing state of shock and grief.

Arlene's base of operations for this and every furlough was the southwest basement corner of her mother's Sioux Center home. In this space Arlene had a bed, dresser, desk, and a rod for hanging clothes. Her parents had built their one-story brick home when they moved off the farm in 1957. Pa had lived here only two years before his heart attack took him. In 1959, Arlene had been in the States on furlough from Nasir, studying for a graduate midwifery certificate at the Frontier Nursing Service in Hyden, Kentucky, when the call about Pa came. Sadly, she did not get home in time to say goodbye. Now, in 1977, Ma still lived in that home on Second Avenue, along with Arlene's sister Grada.

Even though Arlene was not expected to start speaking for several months, the pastor of her home church scheduled her for a ten-minute presentation during both morning services on her first Sunday back. The talk could be simple, he assured her—just answer these three questions:

1. Why did you leave Ethiopia?
2. Were you in danger?
3. What's next?

At 2:00 a.m., Arlene woke up with her pastor's three questions tumbling in her mind. A passage from one of her favorite Bible translations of that era presented itself to her during that early morning hour:

> I have called you back from the ends of the earth and said that you must serve but me alone, for I have chosen you and will not throw you away. Fear not, for I am with you. Do not be dismayed. I am your God. I will strengthen you; I will help you; I will uphold you with my victorious right hand.
>
> (Isaiah 41:9-10 TLB)

She marked this passage for sharing later that morning during the 8:45 and 11:00 services, along with her answers to the questions:

1. Why did you leave Ethiopia?

   I had to leave because the government of Ethiopia required that all schools be taught in Amharic, and I am not a fluent speaker of that language.

2. Were you in danger?

   I was not afraid. But the government is rapidly changing. There were shootings every night in the capital city, so I seldom went out at night. As an American, I was under suspicion. Sometimes, I sensed someone was following me. I've been careful in my lectures during this past year to be medical and never political.

3. What's next?

   I will eventually travel to churches to share what God is doing through the religious revival in Ethiopia. As for a future place of ministry, I will continue to say what I said twenty-six years ago while sitting in that balcony right there: "Here am I, send me."

There were deeper answers she chose not to share that Sunday:

1. Why did you leave Ethiopia?

Ethiopia is experiencing an unpredictable and violent revolution, but if Jesus had said "stay," I would have stayed. However, I had to leave because as a charismatic Christian American, my very presence was a danger to my charismatic Ethiopian friends who are not under the protection of the historic state church.

2. Were you in danger?

I was not afraid in Ethiopia. But whenever I come home, I always experience culture shock, which impacts my emotional well-being. How will I experience the joy of the Lord and the freedom of the Spirit when my heart is elsewhere? I'm not sure I will survive here.

3. What's next?

Well, I'm dreading traveling to my supporting churches, but it's important and I'll do it. I pray that Jesus sends me back overseas, but if he tells me to stay in Sioux Center, I'll do that.

She wished she could say all of it. But she had not yet found the time or the place.

Arlene's calling was to foreign missions. Specifically, her heart's cry was to return to Ethiopia. Her deep encounter with the Holy Spirit had happened there. Her friends in Mettu and Addis Ababa were fellow soldiers in the struggle that was not against flesh and blood but against spiritual wickedness in high places. The believers there were guided by a passionate commitment to Scripture. Along

with the apostle Paul and the church at Philippi, Arlene thanked
her God every time she remembered her east African friends, con-
stantly praying with joy in every one of her prayers for all of them.
As much as she rejoiced in gratitude for them, she was pained by
her absence. To know they were suffering persecution from the
revolutionary government—the "Red Terror"—broke her heart.
Although she dreaded the news concerning Ethiopia, she could
not turn away from it.

Arlene did, however, recognize that her calling was wider than
Ethiopia. She was representing her God, her Schuiteman family,
the First Reformed Church in Sioux Center and its denomination,
her fellow missionaries throughout the world, the church universal,
and finally, Jesus himself in the power of the Spirit for the sake of
the gospel. At fifty-three years old, she expected many more years
of fruitful ministry. Arlene was prepared professionally and spiritu-
ally, ready to obey.

But where should she go and what should she do?

She did not want to take a wrong turn in the next phase of
her missionary journey. She prayed. She fasted. She studied the
Scriptures. She counseled with her pastor and mission leaders. She
wrote countless letters. She took some recreation, but mostly her
typically playful spirit was overcome. Hers was a serious quest, and
there were obstacles that flew in her face. She struggled with those
impediments nearly every day for an entire year.

The day after Henry took Arlene to collect her trunks from
Omaha, Grada was able finally to return to her accounting job at
the Farmer's Co-op. Ma was nearly eighty and required constant
companionship for safety and personal care. A woman named
Adeline served as Ma's attendant, but today was her day off. Now
it was Arlene's turn to discover what Ma's needs demanded. Although those needs were fairly simple, they were unremitting. Ma

could hardly see. Every. Move. Took. Time. She was napping, or she was wandering, which was a potentially dangerous activity because she might fall, leave something open, or forget to turn something off. Ma was often placid and content, but she could suddenly turn needy and frustrated. She was a living exemplar of the end of Jaques's "All the world's a stage" speech in Shakespeare's play *As You Like It*:

> Last scene of all,
> That ends this strange eventful history,
> Is second childishness and mere oblivion,
> Sans teeth, sans eyes, sans taste, sans everything.

What didn't help Ma's routine was that Arlene's reappearance on the scene was an attention magnet. The phone and doorbell rang persistently. Family, friends, and church members wanted to greet the traveler, question her, comfort her, pray with her, and share news of their own lives. The activity was both invigorating and exhausting to Arlene, but it was just plain overwhelming to Ma. In that small house, Ma had little place to escape. Never in her life had Ma wanted to be a burden to another living soul, but the commotion was too much, making Ma sometimes forget who Arlene was and why she and her friends were invading Ma's own home.

Arlene's religious training taught her to honor her father and mother—an easy commandment for Arlene to follow. She had always felt loved by her parents, and she loved them right back. Her love for Ma now doubled, because in loving Ma she was also loving her absent Pa. But who was Ma now? And who was she to her mother? This confusing state of affairs only three weeks into her first month home caused Arlene to write in her journal:

So pathetic—I fought back tears most of the evening.

Ma got progressively crabbier, wandering and muttering,

"I'm the dirty one."
"Did you think this wasn't my house?"
"I want *my* mail."
"I want to go home."

Day after day, the two sisters bathed her, set her hair, sang to her, and prayed with her. Each of the three in her own way was trapped in that little brick house, but their mutual love left them no choice but to press on.

Arlene was a nurse, and her first instinct was to care for any person in need. Now that her mother was so clearly in need, it was a natural impulse for Arlene to wonder if the next mission in life would be to stay right here on Second Avenue for as long as she was needed. She wondered if her foreign missionary days were over. On the first Thursday in April, Arlene went to the midweek service at church. Later that night after Ma was in bed, the sisters had a talk about the future.

Arlene said, "I'm thinking about what to tell the mission board."

Grada asked, "About where to go?"

"About whether to go."

"What would you do if you didn't go?"

"Stay here and help you with Ma."

Grada shook her head. "No. You're just seeing it up close. But nothing's changed. You have your mission."

Arlene pushed back. "But isn't she getting worse? Already it takes both of us to care for her. Should I even be thinking about going on my deputation tour, let alone going overseas?"

Grada smiled. "Too many questions. First, no offense, but she's worse because you're here. You come with a lot of hubbub, you know."

"I know. I'm sorry."

"Not your fault," said Grada, then added, "Besides, it's not just *your* mission."

That response made the tears well up, because Arlene knew how true this statement was. Grada had mimeographed, addressed, and licked stamps for thousands of prayer letters. She had attended umpteen church services to show Arlene's slides. By now, Grada nearly had the script memorized. Plus, she was certainly not alone. At how many family devotions after how many meals in how many houses for how many years had Arlene's name been spoken in the prayers of young and old? For Arlene to withdraw from foreign missions would subtract something profound and precious from a multitude. She could step back, but she had better be certain that she was called to do so.

"What would Pa want?" asked Grada.

They both knew the answer to that question. And they believed that Ma, on her best days, still wanted the same. The decisions made that night would sustain them when Ma's days got worse. And they did. In early June, she fell getting out of bed. At the time, she weighed only eighty-seven pounds, which may have contributed to her not breaking any bones. But the fall seemed to impact her movements and disposition for weeks. By autumn, Ma was not sleeping well, sometimes waking up five times in the night, calling for help. Then, in early winter, her incontinence began.

Ma was not the only one struggling with physical limitations. During her furlough year, headaches sometimes laid Arlene low for hours or even a whole day. The pain might beset her during the day or awaken her at the night. It nauseated her. She used shorthand with Grada: "I have a wet-cloth headache," for example, meant Arlene was going to lie down with a cold washcloth across her brow, trying to sleep off the pain.

From the time Arlene arrived home, she noted in her journal approximately one bad headache a month. She sometimes called them "malaria headaches," knowing they might be symptomatic of malaria or malaria medication still lurking in her bloodstream. If that was the case, the headaches would naturally dissipate if she waited them out.

She also wondered if the headaches were indications of sinus trouble. But because the trouble receded relatively quickly each time, she dismissed each episode until the next one arose. Consequently, nothing was done except to endure.

Arlene's body could have been reflecting what was going on in her emotions. Although she had expected culture shock after having been away from Iowa for four years, the quantity of products in every store surprisingly stunned her—and she was amazed at the size of the stores themselves and how the shopping malls seemed to have gotten bigger and bigger. When she learned the price tag for the fireworks that her hometown exploded in fifteen minutes on the Fourth of July, she wrote the word *Waste* in her journal and underlined it in bold. That same day, she wrote,

Loneliness, homesickness, and grief hit me again, and I can do nothing about it.

Before long, Arlene was experiencing some degree of depression, but her upbringing had not taught her to seek professional help for a mental condition. She was raised to value self-reliance. If self-reliant people were sad, then they should "snap out of it." Sometimes her religious culture even spiritualized emotional distress, naming sadness "the power of darkness" with the remedy to "put on the whole armor of God." The situation was complex because the strategies commended in Paul's letter to the Ephesians were good strategies, especially for Arlene who knew what it meant to "pray in the Spirit on all occasions with all kinds of prayers" (Ephesians 6:18a NIV). However, professional assistance might have been needful as well.

Some of Arlene's circle grew concerned, and a few even commented to her that she seemed depressed. Her pastor went so far as to recommend that she consider a psychological evaluation. She chose not to. Her self-prescribed medication was threefold: spend time with Jesus every day, just get through this year, and return to the mission field. If she could accomplish these three, then she believed she would get better. So she ran to her Savior early in the morning. When things got worse, she got up earlier, sometimes writing her prayers, such as this one in April 1977:

Lord, teach me to love the way through the night. Teach me to wait endlessly until the distress and darkness have been transformed and Your promise is fulfilled. Teach me to love You in the dark until Your Love illumines the way.

At the end of September, her speaking tour began, and as tiring as it was, her public face and private faith remained strong. Midway through the tour, at her sister Milly's home in Holland, Michigan, she prayed:

Jesus, I invite You to come sit with me where I am now, to enter into all that is happening concerning this deputation trip, concerning what's happening to my Ethiopian family, concerning the working out of Your plan for me. You are the Good Shepherd, My Guide. I want to be a conqueror, an overcomer. Maybe I don't know what this involves or what I'm asking You, but You know all things. You know that I love You.

Arlene's supervisor, Glenn, suggested a deadline of Thanksgiving for making a decision about her return to the field. Together, they considered the available options. Frontier Nursing Service

(FNS) in Kentucky, Arlene's midwifery alma mater, had heard she was home on furlough. In a phone call, they flung the door wide open. She could work in the wards, teach, or even take classes. She was more than welcome to return. Another site option was Oman, where a teaching position was available. This was the mission once led by Dr. Paul Harrison, whose call to medical ministry had so stirred Arlene's heart back during the 1944 Orange City mission festival when she first felt God leading her overseas. To move to Muskat, Oman, would bring Arlene's journey full circle. But she gently held off both Kentucky and the Arabian Peninsula. As far as she was concerned, the door to Ethiopia was not yet completely closed. She needed to be sure.

Arlene scoured the newspapers and magazines for glimmers of hope, but Chairman Mengistu in Ethiopia offered none. The leader of the Derg government tightened his grip. In his speeches, he threatened death to all enemies of the state, making his point by waving "bloody" handkerchiefs and smashing bottles filled with red paint. Mengistu's Communist movement openly allied with the Soviet Union, and most American government officials were given only a few days to leave the country. United States Major James Rust reported the trauma of having to shoot his family's dogs so they would not be left to roam the streets of Addis Ababa. Missionary Aviation Fellowship flew its planes home to the United States.

Then one Tuesday, a fellow missionary called Arlene to let her know that Presbyterian missionary Don McClure had been murdered by Somali bandits who had crossed into Ethiopia during the security breach of those troubled times. Ethiopia's stability was being shattered.

As the news kept coming, Arlene's family, home church, and denomination discouraged any further consideration of her return to Ethiopia. Arlene still sought God's will. She trusted that God would eventually speak to her personally through Scripture, prayer, fasting, and the counsel of fellow believers. There was no one whose attentiveness to the Spirit she trusted more than the mature believers of the Mettu church in Ethiopia, so she wrote to them. Many of them wrote back to her. Their faith was strong, and their tone was friendly. But she began to notice a certain reserve in their communications. She eventually learned that the Protestant churches of the western mountains were being closed by the government. Some letters from Ethiopia were written with hidden meanings, like this short note from her dear friend Iteffa, the evangelist.

Dear Miss Arlene,

> *Greetings in the name of our Lord Jesus.*
> *I am writing you this letter to just urge that you take a special time with the Lord to pray for us. I am here in A/A, but quite strange things are going on with our work there at our working place.*
> *Tomorrow, I am going back. I don't really know what will happen to me. I don't have much to say. (Acts 20:22–24 . . . 25?) Praise the Lord!!*
> *May the Lord give us another time to share our blessing after our suffering. The name "Jesus" is saving power through faith in God. Amen.*
> *Remember Seyoum and Tadessa are already in.*
>
> *Your Brother*

This short note meant that the leaders of the churches in the western mountains were in desperate straits. Seyoum and Tadessa were in jail and likely being tortured. Iteffa was returning home, and he was well aware that as a leader in the church, he would likely be arrested. It was common during the days of the Derg for prisoners to be packed into small cells, shoulder to shoulder with no furniture. Any sleeping or even sitting would have to be on the floor and in shifts. Food, water, and sanitation were all doubtful. Iteffa referenced Paul's farewell to the elders at Ephesus to communicate to Arlene that "chains and afflictions await me." He was asserting, with Paul, his faith in "the ministry I have received from the Lord Jesus." But his hesitant inclusion of verse 25 was a warning: "Now I know that none of you among whom I have gone about preaching the kingdom will ever see me again."

There was one final message Arlene was waiting to hear from her Ethiopian friends: *Come back.* But that message never came. She concluded that they were concerned for her safety and that she was a danger to them. The answer was clear. As long as Mengistu ruled in Ethiopia, she should not go back.

A letter from Glenn arrived asking Arlene to itemize the value of the personal property she had lost in Ethiopia so he could request reimbursement. Arlene wrote in reply that any loss was her thank offering for the privilege of having served there. With that, the Ethiopian chapter of Arlene's African mission was officially closed.

With the Thanksgiving deadline upon her, Arlene asked Glenn if she might say yes to Kentucky, working for a few months at the modern hospital there and learning current midwifery practices. Glenn readily agreed and so did the staff at FNS. She arranged to leave Sioux Center after the holidays. On December 31, she wrote,

> *It was a wilderness journey this year. A year of healing and adjustments. A year of being weaned from Ethiopian friends. "And you know how He has cared for you again and again here in the wilderness, just as a Father cares for His child."*
> [Deuteronomy 1:31 TLB]

At that point, Arlene did not have a plan or know God's will for the next step in her missionary journey. But the step had been in the works since April 5, 1976. On that day, when Arlene was still in Addis Ababa, Ethiopia, she had received a phone call from a Jeannie Byer.

"I don't know if you remember me."

"Oh, my! Are you Jeannie Jordan?"

"That's right. You have an amazing memory."

"How many—twenty years? You were a girl."

"At Nasir. Yes."

"Where are you calling from?"

"Right here. The airport. My husband, Dave, is a doctor at Mayo, and we're flying through to Zambia on a short-term. But we'd love to take you to dinner and catch up. May we?"

"Right now? Of course, but let me treat you. Can you get a taxi to the Tiki National Restaurant?"

"We'll do that. But you should know that Dave will never let you—"

"We'll see. I'll start out right now. How are your parents? Never mind—we'll talk at the restaurant."

Arlene briefly noted the event in her journal. She simply wrote,

Dr. Dave and Jeannie Byer and I went to Tuki National Restaurant for injera ba wat [flatbread with meat] *at night.*

A year and a half later, in December 1977, Dr. Dave Byer learned that the tutor at Macha Nurses Training School in Zambia would be leaving the following summer. He thought immediately of the teacher he had met in Addis Ababa, and he sent a letter recommending Arlene to Reverend Earl Musser, director of Missions Overseas for the Brethren in Christ Church.

When Reverend Musser returned to his office from Christmas break, he opened Dave's letter and immediately wrote to Arlene. He put his letter in the mail on January 3, 1978, addressed to the brick house on Second Avenue in Sioux Center, Iowa. But by the time his letter arrived in Iowa, Arlene had already left for Kentucky.

2

Labor

Bulyebulye tabulyeeti bweta aawuputa.
Good things come from hard work.

---

*Has the wilderness journey come to an end? Make
me strong and firm, burning with love, burning with
dedication for You, with one aim only: I want Jesus,
nothing but Jesus. I want no relief of any hardship; I
do not want the comfort of seeing and feeling—I want
only to embrace You in faith, and love You, Jesus—in
darkness and temptation.*

January 1, 1978

On Saturday, January 7, Arlene traveled the new Daniel Boone
Parkway (later renamed the Hal Rogers Parkway), taking the turn-
off at Thousandsticks in Kentucky. She was exhilarated to once again
travel Highway 118 and the final four miles through a wooded pass
into Hyden. It was a sunny day and unseasonably warm.

Arriving at the Frontier Nursing Service (FNS), she parked her
car next to the barn, a remnant of when Mary Breckinridge came to
this valley in the Appalachian Mountains in 1925 to provide medical
care to the impoverished people of rural Kentucky. In those early
days, the FNS staff of midwives rode horses to otherwise inacces-
sible cabins tucked in the forested hills that blanket the southeastern
third of Kentucky. Even now, Arlene could recall the warm barn
smells she had first known back in 1959 when she took her turn at
cleaning stalls and pitching manure. The horses and their familiar

odors were gone now, and the barn had been renovated into apartments. Room 7 would be Arlene's home for the next few months. Her apartment was a single room furnished with a bed, dresser, desk, and easy chair. Another nurse shared the bathroom, accessing it by a door opposite to Arlene's.

The day after Arlene arrived, the steep road up to the barn turned to ice and snow; she would not move her car for the next eight weeks. She could manage on foot between her apartment and the maternity wards and even into town for groceries. This place had certainly changed during her two decades away, but she was grateful to be where she could heal and grow and listen for God's call. It was so good to be back at the work she knew and loved. The FNS teaching hospital was glad to add a nurse with Arlene's experience, even if only for a few months. The situation was a win-win for everyone. Arlene's paycheck was forwarded to the Reformed Church office since the Mission Board continued paying her salary even though her furlough year had ended.

"Oh no! You get hurt?" asked Barbara from her hospital bed.

"I'm fine," Arlene replied. "Totally my fault. It's been a whole year since I've done I.V. needles—I'm out of practice. It's just a pricked finger."

"I'm done with this bed here if you wanna lie down."

Arlene laughed. "Every time I had to take a sliver out for my pa back on the farm, he pretended I had pricked his finger terribly and he'd give a shout to startle me."

"He was a tease?"

"Yes. If I'd ever really hurt him, he wouldn't have let on."

"He seems right nice."

"Yes, he was. But he died when I was working here at this very hospital—I mean at the old hospital before this new one was built. My sister Grada had to call me with the news."

"Where he live?"

"Up in the state of Iowa. Sioux Center is the name of the town."

"That where you was born and raised?"

"Yes."

"What made you come here?"

"I went to midwifery school here, about twenty years ago. So I came back to learn the new techniques."

"Yer not gunna stay?"

"I've spent most of my working days in Africa. I'm waiting to hear about work there."

"Well, you should stay here. Kentucky is good as Africa."

"I'll tell you what, Barbara. When you go into labor—and you will—I'll be here to meet your baby."

Barbara sighed. "Seem like it ain't never gunna happen. The medicine you put in my arm wun't no good."

"It doesn't work on everybody."

"Sure din't work on me. Now I getta walk out with a baby inside."

"Give it a few more days. Would you like me to pray with you before you go?"

"Yes, ma'am."

When Barbara returned in early February for another try at inducing labor, Arlene was on call. With her shift about over, a patient in active labor showed up at 11:00 p.m. Arlene stayed to help one of the student nurses with this—her very first admission. Arlene went home for some rest, which turned out to be needful because the next day turned into a sixteen-hour shift. The girl from the previous night had delivered safely at some point late in the shift, much to the joy of a dozen family members who ignored visitor rules and crowded into the room, creating what Arlene described in her journal as "Bedlam."

That night, back in the barn, exhausted as she was, she listened all the way through First and Second Peter on tape to calm herself down. She had a suspicion she had grown too old to be an on-call nurse in a maternity ward. Three hours later, she was up again. The Scripture verse that came to her mind was from Psalm 32:8: "I will instruct thee and teach thee in the way which thou shalt go." Arlene wrote to herself,

God is saying that this place where you are now is a temporary assignment. He is showing you that this kind of work schedule is too much for you.

Too much, yes, but John G. Schuiteman's daughter was not a quitter. Arlene hustled down to the hospital and learned that Barbara had finally started to labor and had a Pit Drip going. Pitocin administered intravenously was strong medicine that typically evoked the onset of contractions within thirty minutes. Barbara was indeed experiencing contractions, so this time Arlene would stay until the end.

She stayed at Barbara's side all morning, finally taking a twenty-minute break at 1:30 p.m. Later that afternoon, the time finally arrived. The ward supervisor, Bernadette, encouraged Arlene to do the delivery herself. She would have preferred to let the supervisor take the lead, but after encouragement, she set to work.

The diagnosis indicated the need for a right medio-lateral episiotomy, reminding Arlene of the double episiotomy she had performed on an Arab mother back in Nasir. That surgery had been necessitated by culturally practiced FGM (Female Genital Mutilation—a case in which the vagina has been sewed nearly shut). Barbara's episiotomy was necessitated by the baby's size, likely the result of the extra-long pregnancy. But the episiotomy did not fully solve the problem. Far from it. The progress of labor was still too slow. Arlene asked for the vacuum extractor. Barbara pushed while Arlene pulled, and suddenly the head came through, along with an arm and a shoulder. Arlene's large and practiced hands felt through the mess of tissue and fluid to find the baby's neck. There it was, that ancient danger—the umbilical cord around the infant's throat.

The conduit that had sustained life for all those months was now threatening to take it away. Arlene had mere seconds to act. But she had been on this road before. She pressed the child back toward its mother with one hand while using the other hand to slip the cord over the baby's head, setting it free.

"Now push, Barbara. Push."

"Yes, ma'am."

In short order, a living boy was born. His weight told the story of his stubborn entry: nine pounds, fifteen ounces.

Still the work was not done. Just as she had done late one night in an Arab home near the northern bank of the Sobat River, she sutured Barbara's episiotomy in the Mary Breckinridge Hospital near the western bank of the Middle Fork Kentucky River. After surgery, she sat down to update the charts. It had been another long day.

Late that night, Arlene pulled out her journal and wrote this entry:

Home at 11 p.m. I praise God for the strength He gave me. It was absolutely supernatural. Thanks for Bernadette, Ida May, Molly Lee, and J. K. God led me through a hard day when my own mental, physical, and emotional strength was gone.

3

Home

Kunkombokombo nkukwanu.
Where your umbilical cord was cut and buried,
there is your home.

Praise, my soul, the King of Heaven!
Ye behold Him face to face!
Saints triumphant bow before Him,
Gathered in from every race!

Hallelujah! Oh God when? Mold me and make me a
triumphant saint.
    Good service: "An Agenda for Lent." I'm
anticipating real spiritual blessings this Easter
season. Snowing and very dark today. Wrote
several letters.
    Still no peace about not answering Legesse's
letters. He'll no doubt think I did not receive them.

February 5, 1978

Having flown out of Addis Ababa on February 1, 1977, Arlene
was now moving past her one-year-anniversary phase of grieving
her departure from Ethiopia. She could no longer think, "Last year
at this time, I was doing [fill in the blank] in Addis Ababa."

It was much longer than a year since she had given her final
answer to the Ethiopian suitor who had begged for her hand in marriage. Even so, after all this time, he wrote to her. She did not reply.

He had sent a letter to her family that apparently got lost amid the unreliability of Ethiopian infrastructure. His most recent missive was a Christmas card that made it through. Arlene had not sent him a card, nor did she answer his.

It was in Kentucky that Arlene finally faced the task head on. On the Sunday prior to the start of Lent, she pulled out a piece of blank airmail stationary. After some pleasant salutary greetings and best wishes, she wrote the following:

> *Legesse, you must forget me. Last week on Wednesday, it was one year that I left your country. When I remember it makes me sad.*
>
> *On January 5 I left my home and began to work in a hospital in Kentucky. It is far from my Mother's home but it is God's plan for me to work here around three months or as God says. Maybe I will go to work in another country sometime but that is not clear.*
>
> *This place where I am is somewhat like Ethiopia. I have a room in a place where other nurses are living. There is quite a good church and pastor. Soon we will have Bible class about the work of the Holy Spirit. God is blessing me in my spiritual life here.*
>
> *Please do not answer this letter. First I was not going to answer you, but I thought you might not know if I received your Christmas card.*
>
> *"May mercy, peace, and love be multiplied to you." (Jude 1:2)*
>
> *And I pray that God will bless your ministry. He is coming and preparing all things in heaven.*

She had drawn an international line between them, referring to Ethiopia as "your country" and Sioux Center as "my home." In her journal, she wrote,

> *Oh God . . . not sure what else to say.*

4

Mail

Bulaama chaacha.
Days bring different things.

On "Day Call" and Ellen H., 31, G9 in labor at 8 a.m.
Sandy H. (FN3 student) on. She does well, her 10th one
today. Pt with Hx PPHx3 etc. On Pit Drip 10:30-12:30
then delivered living female. All went well. PTL. Nurse
Midwives Mtg 3-6 p.m. Ate supper at Hosp. 7 letters and
Time Magazine today.

March 8, 1978

Early on Wednesday, March 8, Arlene received a call to the
Hyden hospital to oversee the labor of Ellen, a thirty-one-year-
old in her ninth Gravida (pregnancy). Sandy, the Frontier Nursing
Service student midwife that day, was marking a special milestone.
She needed ten deliveries before she could graduate, and today was
the day. Ellen had a history of postpartum hemorrhaging (she had
experienced bleeding after three of her prior deliveries). After only
minimal contractions by 10:30 a.m., Arlene approved adding Pitocin
to Ellen's I.V., which brought on strong contractions within a couple
of hours. Finally, a healthy baby girl was born and Ellen was stable.
"Praise the Lord!" Arlene proclaimed in her journal entry above.

The remainder of Arlene's arduous day was taken up with a
three-hour meeting, which left little time to prepare supper so she
ate in the hospital cafeteria. On her way to the horse barn, she

stopped at the mail room and was delighted to discover a magazine and seven letters—a number significant enough to earn a special mention in her journal.

Back in Sioux Center, Grada was an expert at monitoring Arlene's flow of mail. Grada knew which letters to forward immediately and which ones to stash in the basement bureau drawer. She kept the family round-robin letters circulating and was faithful in distributing Arlene's prayer letter to the churches.

Mail was Arlene's vital connection to the world at large. The telephone was too expensive to be used except for emergencies. Besides using mail to communicate with denomination and medical administrators, mail was also crucial to Arlene's emotional well-being, a bulwark against future culture shock. The more she could keep up with family activities back home, the less bumpy her reentry would be when she returned.

Arlene also used mail to fuel her own spiritual life and prayer disciplines. The Bible was her primary source of divine revelation, but she also believed that God used mail. Here are snippets of the letters and corresponding journal entries that, by the spring and summer of 1978, reveal Arlene's discernment of her next missionary call.

January 1. Arlene's letter to her supporting churches:

> *Recently, the way opened up for me to spend a few months working on the staff and faculty of the School of Midwifery and Family Nursing in Hyden, Kentucky. This is a <u>temporary furlough</u> assignment for me.*

January 10. Letter to Arlene from Rev. Musser, Brethren in Christ Church Missions, Elizabethtown, Pennsylvania:

Dr. and Mrs. David Byer have given us your name. By next summer we will need a tutor to head up our nurses' training program at Macha, Zambia mission hospital. We would be happy to hear from you as to whether or not you have any interest.

January 12. Arlene's letter to Rev. Musser:

I met Dr. and Mrs. Byer in Addis Ababa on one of their trips to Zambia, and I have known Jeannie for a long time. I would like to know some more about your nurse's program. I am sure my letter reveals my sincere interest in serving Christ in Zambia if that is where the Lord calls me.

January 26. Arlene's letter to her family:

At this point I still have no idea about where I'll serve after FNS. Time will tell. There has been a letter from a mission in Zambia asking if I was interested in teaching in their school of nursing. I've written to ask some questions.

January 29. Letter to Arlene from Rev. Glenn Bruggers, Reformed Church in America Missions, Grandville, Michigan:

I appreciate the copy of your letter from the Brethren in Christ Mission and feel you have asked very pertinent questions. I hope each day in Hyden will prove exciting, satisfying, and make you feel completely in His care.

February 4. Letter to Arlene from Dr. Dave Byer, Mayo Clinic, Rochester, Minnesota:

I took the liberty of mentioning your name to Rev. Musser as I knew he was looking for a nursing instructor for the Macha Zambia Enrolled Nurse School. I'm sorry. I should have gotten a letter off to you telling you I was going to do this. I note with interest you are working with FNS. Several other of our Macha midwives have trained there.

February 6. Letter to Arlene from Rev. Musser:

Thanks for your letter of January 12. Dave and Jeannie Byer are good persons. I am glad to share with you some information about our mission (under separate cover). We will send application forms to you if you desire. We'll pray that the Lord will lead you into that which is His will.

February 14. Arlene's journal entry:

Wrote to Musser that the packet had not arrived yet. News tonight says Ethiopia is breaking diplomatic relations with America, Britain, and West Germany. Spent a long time praying for Mettu Christians by name. Couldn't sleep.

February 20. Letter to Arlene from Dave Byer:

You probably have gathered that the Macha hospital is about 40 miles in the country from Choma. Being away from town has the advantage of providing less distraction for the students. I like Chief Macha and respect him despite his drinking problem and polygamy problem.

February 20. Arlene's journal entry:

Lord, please let me not become anxious, nor push ahead, or drag behind as You lead the way. Keep me from complaining.

February 23. Arlene's journal entry:

I feel so lonely, so longing for the place to settle and know it is God's spot for me. God's Word today: "I will cause the shower to come down in his season; there shall be showers of blessing" [Ezekiel 34:26b KJV]. *I yield my life to the God of peace. I offer myself as a living sacrifice.*

March 1. Arlene's journal entry:

Long Distant call from Mr. Musser. Information mailed still hasn't arrived, so he will send duplicates. God, is this Your leading?

March 10. Arlene's journal entry:

Walked trail to my rock. Beautiful thawing day.

[Note: The rock was a large flat boulder, up the hill past the old mine entrance. Wherever she lived, Arlene looked for an outdoor chapel for reading, writing, and praying. This rock had been her Hyden chapel since 1959 when she ran there and threw herself prone the moment she learned of Pa's heart attack.]

March 11. Arlene's letter to Glenn Bruggers:

Mr. Musser's packet of information about Zambia has been lost in the mail. I have been more isolated here than in Africa. But it has been a necessary experience.

March 15. Letter to Arlene from Eleanor Vandevort (Vandy), a Sudan missionary colleague living at this time in Wenham, Massachusetts:

I hope your life in the Horse Barn is quiet and strengthening tonight. Our storm is still here in the fact of snow yet unmoved and unmelted. The land is still under its blanket. People here wonder if there will be spring. I believe there will! The mourning doves are singing now, and the chickadees are giving their mating call. God will send spring even as He sent winter.

God has brought us a fine rector. He is a godly man. He believes that our first responsibility is prayer. He keeps this ever before us.

March 21. Letter to Arlene from Glenn Bruggers:

If you haven't received Mr. Musser's promised package, please feel free to telephone him. Charge the call to us. Strange to realize how isolated one can be in the middle of a country that boasts of its transportation and communications.

March 22. Arlene's journal entry:

Went up to the Rock to wait upon God, just to be quiet in His presence. Cleansed of fears and doubts. Basking in His love and the healing of the Sun of Righteousness. Prayed deeply in tongues, God's Spirit within me making the requests I haven't known how to make. Reread Bruggers letter.

March 23. Letter to Arlene from Leatta Weidenbach, Ethiopia missionary colleague on furlough in Avon, South Dakota:

I'm sure that working in a U.S. hospital is overwhelming! With the new equipment, etc., etc., etc.

It is most interesting that you have an invitation to the Macha Hospital in Zambia. I did visit that hospital. It's about 4–5 hours by road out of Lusaka.

I finally told them I'd come to Katete. The Lord is going to have a lot of gifts to supply for that. I'm sure the Lord will lead you to the right place.

March 24. Arlene's journal entry:

Good Friday. I will fast today in memory of Jesus' sufferings. Phoned Rev. Musser to talk about Macha, Zambia. He will send application form. Also phoned Jeannie Byer. Is God leading in the direction of Zambia???

March 24. Letter to Arlene from Glenn Bruggers:

The school for Zambia Enrolled Nurses in Macha is in the southern province, 200 miles from Lusaka, the capital. There are 73 tribal groups in the country. The Tonga are the main tribe near Macha. The setting is rural. The school was started about ten years ago. It is one of sixteen such schools approved by the General Nursing Council of Zambia. In many ways it seems VERY MUCH like Mettu although this program may be a wee bit more sophisticated.

March 29. Arlene's journal entry:

"We must not suffer Satan to shake our confidence in the God of truth by pointing to our unanswered prayers. Delays are not denials. Unanswered petitions are not unheard." [Arlene placed the quotation marks but neglected to cite the source: Charles Spurgeon.] *A long talk with Bernadette. If I wanted to stay, I could take a course at Booth and qualify for American College of Nurse-Midwives. But I don't think God's plan for me is to be married to midwifery and FNS.*

March 30. Letter to Arlene from Rev. Musser:

We have an opening at our school at Macha Hospital, which is available this late summer. We are glad to enclose application forms for you. Thanks for considering service with us in BIC Missions. We'll pray together that the Lord will make known his will for you at this time.

March 30. Arlene's journal entry:

Walked up the trail a little while and wrote several letters. Application forms for BICM for Zambia arrived. Is this the way, Lord? All my feelings and indications are positive. Will wait and pray until after trip to General Program Council [Reformed Church in America meeting the following week].

March 31. Arlene's journal entry:

Appt. with Rev. Hood to discuss latest developments so that he may pray.

April 6. Arlene's journal entry:

Flew to Chicago, GPC meeting. Long talk with Glenn who supports my application for Zambia. I'm to proceed. He will call Mr. Musser.

[Note: Arlene left GPC early to attend a family wedding in Iowa. She remained home for the weekend.]

April 9. Arlene's journal entry:

To 350th celebration of the Dutch Reformed Church in America. I was called to tell congregation of persecution in Ethiopia. Have headache all day.

April 10. Arlene's letter to her extended family:

I've been surprised that Mom looks so good. She may have slowed down a bit and Grada says that she thinks she ought not go to church anymore and I tend to agree.

I had a good time in Chicago and was able to talk with board executives about the possibility of applying for the position in Zambia with the Brethren in Christ Mission there. They approved. I would rather that you did not talk to others about this yet. Just continue to pray.

I'm going to have coffee with Rev. and Mrs. Rynbrandt so I must stop now and get this in the mail.

April 10. Arlene's journal entry:

Went to talk with Rev. and Mrs. Rynbrandt about the possibility of going to Zambia. They approve too.

April 13. Arlene's letter to Rev. Musser:

I returned to Hyden yesterday evening after my trip to our General Program Council meeting in Crete, Illinois. I was able to talk with Glenn Bruggers and others of our mission staff. All of them were in agreement about my applying for the post in Zambia and believed that this was God's leading for me.

I also went on to my home in Iowa to attend a wedding of my niece. At that time I had an opportunity to talk with our pastor and my family. They were also in agreement.

It is hard for me not to convey my excitement over the possibility of serving in Zambia. However, I am well aware that God can close the way or open it wide so I continue to wait upon Him.

April 13. Arlene's journal entry:

Today I filled out application for work in Macha, Zambia and mailed it. Walked up to rock and meditated.

[Note: On the application, she wrote her statement of faith: *I believe in the Triune God: Father, Son, and Holy Spirit, and in the Bible as the Holy and inspired word of God. I believe that Jesus died for me, that His blood washes away my sin, and that by faith in His death and resurrection I am assured of Eternal life in heaven. This is not because of any merit of my own but because of what Jesus accomplished for me.*]

April 15. Arlene's journal entry:

> *Woke up rested and feeling so good. Brkf. Washed out stockings. Then hurried up trail to read and pray. Finished reading book of Joshua. "You know very well that God's promises to you have all come true" [Joshua 23:14b TLB]. My spirit worships God in this quiet beautiful spot. The very peace of the Spirit is here, the beauty of the redbud, dogwood, myriad shades of green in a variety of trees, the soft gentle breeze, the warm rays of the Sun of Righteousness who has brought healing in His wings—Amen! Hallelujah!—the pure blue sky and puffy clouds, His Word my manna. This is like arriving in the land of Canaan after a wilderness journey.*

April 20. Letter to Arlene from Leatta:

> *The hospital at Macha is fairly new. ZENs (Zambia Enrolled Nurses) are being trained at Macha. I'm sure you could handle it beautifully.*
>
> *Katete is quite a ways from Macha. Macha is about 4 hrs. by road west of Lusaka—about half the way down to Livingstone and the Falls. Katete is on the Great East Road near to Chipata on the Malawian border. Katete is Anglican. They have an 80+ yr-old priest. They "say even song" each day. I think the attendance is about three.*
>
> *CMAZ is Churches Medical Association of Zambia. All church hospitals work together under it, and they would be the ones to process all your papers.*
>
> *Yes, I know how hard it is to leave a mother who desperately needs your help. I thought we had my Mom all settled, and then another barrage of searchings for the Lord's will.*

April 27. Arlene's journal entry:

> *"God, even our own God"* [Psalm 67:6 KJV]. *He is the Sun through the darkness, He is my shield against the enemy, He is my Guide in this maze of life. And I still have no assurance of the future—no answer about Zambia.*

Arlene didn't yet know that she was being spoken of in Zambia. In April, a woman from the Churches Medical Association of Zambia wrote to Leatta who forwarded the letter to Arlene.

May 1. Letter to Leatta from Sylvia Chesterman:

> *The purpose of writing this letter is to take up the issue of your friend. We had provisionally hoped she would go to St. Francis* [the name of the hospital in Katete] *as the tutor. We felt this was a real answer to prayer. The staffing situation at St. Francis is far more acute than Macha. Please contact your friend for me and ask her to consider this.*

May 2. Cable to Rev. Musser from Rev. Sterns, Brethren in Christ Church Mission, Lusaka, Zambia:

> *ARLENE SCHUITEMAN IS WANTED AT KATETE HOSPITAL. APPLICATION HAS NOT BEEN MADE. LEATTA WEIDENBACH DEFINITELY RECRUITED FOR KATETE.*

May 2. Arlene's journal entry:

> *Mr. Musser phoned at 9 a.m. He said he received a cable from Zambia saying, "Arlene Schuiteman is wanted at Katete Hospital." He said that they are assigning Barbara Peterson to Macha since she applied first. This door to Macha is closed for some reason. Headache and heavy disappointed feeling.*

Walked up trail to pray. Binding spirit of heaviness and fear. Lifted and free at 5 p.m.

May 11. Letter to Arlene from Leatta:

Just want to answer your questions as you pray about Katete. The MD in charge is British—a fellow of the Royal College of Surgeons. Very pleasant and I thought good with the patients, considerate of them. Also I thought steady personality—seemed not easily ruffled up and upset with little happenings (like an attempted thieving they had at the pharmacy the night I was there).

May 24. Letter to Arlene from Sylvia Chesterman (there is some confusion, as she does not seem to be aware that the Macha position was filled):

I am thankful to have received your address from Leatta this week. I am sorry for the situation you now find yourself in with a difficult decision to make.

Macha Mission Hospital has invited you to be the tutor in their enrolled nurse training school. There is also a great need for your help in a similar capacity at St. Francis Hospital in Katete where Leatta will also be working.

We must leave you to make the decision as you feel led.

May 25. Arlene's letter to Sylvia Chesterman:

I believe that God is leading me back to Africa. If the Katete school is similar to the one described to me at Macha, then I do believe I am qualified and will be doing what I love to do. However, Leatta indicated that the hospital is 300+ beds and the school has 60+ students. My concern is that this is too large a load for one person. Or are there additional teaching staff?

Arlene asked Sylvia a myriad of additional questions about the curriculum, housing, and life in that region. Since mail seemed to take about two weeks to travel each way, she took the liberty of including a résumé. She finished the letter by writing,

I know that God will either open or close this door for service according to His will and plan.

She sent a copy of the letter to Glenn, saying that she was eager for his response.

Arlene was not interested in falling prey to want or even need. She would not say yes to Katete solely because of their wanting her. That rationale would be, in her assessment, prideful. Neither would she say yes because the need was acute. That method of discernment would be chaotic because there are always needs. Step by step was her method, trusting that her Shepherd would use both rod and staff to guide and guard.

On Sunday, June 4, Leatta telephoned. "Arlene, please don't worry about the expense. It's only a matter of weeks now, and I can't depend on the mail anymore. I'll ask Glenn if he'll pay for this call, but anyway, you won't have to."

"It's good to hear from you. Thanks for all the letters."

"I'll write again as soon as I hear from Faith Cairns. The mail takes so long, and then things get crossed up and all confused. I asked her for specifics on Zambian nurses' uniforms. I've heard that they're very specific about—"

"Leatta, I'm not sure I'm going to Katete."

"Oh, I'm so sorry. Did Macha change their mind?"

"No. That's closed. But I haven't even received an application to fill out for Katete."

Leatta laughed. "Did they offer you a position?"

"Well . . . Sylvia said the decision was up to me."

"That means they offered you the job! Did they tell you which job?"

"I'm not positive, but I think it's the tutor."

"Oh! Thank you, Lord! I was afraid they were going to ask me to be the tutor. You're the one for that. I'll help in any way you want. But you're the tutor."

On June 8, a letter from Leatta arrived with a long list of specifics for the Zambian nurses' uniform. The country's motto was "One Zambia, One Nation," and that mentality informed the clothing of medical professionals. The dresses were to be a simple style in a fine, white drill fabric. Arlene was told *not* to have them made in the United States but to purchase them when she landed in Lusaka. She should, however, purchase the accessories to the dress uniform ahead of time, because no one could be certain as to the availability of other goods in Lusaka. Caps were to be lacy. The tutor's cap was to be frilly. Stockings and lace-up shoes were to be brown. The floor of the nation was, after all, dusty, so feet and legs covered in brown would help hide that fact. Cardigans were also necessary since the temperatures did drop, and the sweaters could be either blue or gray. On June 10, Arlene wrote in her journal,

> *Our defeats can also lead us to a deeper revelation of God's love.*

Reading Hannah Hurnard's allegorical book *Mountains of Spices*, Arlene noted with joy the lyrics of a mountain song about a journey similar to her own:

> *In acceptance lieth peace,*
>   *O my heart be still;*
> *Let thy restless worries cease*
>   *And accept his will.*
> *Though this test be not thy choice,*
> *It is his—therefore rejoice.*

In his plan there cannot be
Aught to make thee sad:
If this is his choice for thee,
Take it and be glad.
Make from it some lovely thing
To the glory of thy King.

Cease from sighs and murmuring
Sing his loving grace,
This thing means thy furthering
To a wealthy place.
From thy fears he'll give release,
In acceptance lieth peace.

On June 15, she invested in a long-distance call to New York. She spoke with Glenn, and he affirmed taking steps toward Katete. He promised to write to CMAZ urging a timely reply as to the next step in the process that would make Arlene's status definite. In the meantime, Arlene got busy collecting every possible document that might be asked of her. If and when anything shifted into high gear, she would be ready.

June 22. Letter to Arlene from Dr. James Cairns, St. Francis Hospital, Katete, Zambia:

> *After discussion with senior members of the nursing staff and Sylvia Chesterman, we feel that it is right to offer you the post of Principal Tutor.*

June 22. Arlene's journal entry:

> *I got two letters from Zambia today, including all the forms to fill out and a list of papers to send!!! They ask me to be the Principal Tutor!*

God, I take this step in faith that it is Your will.

June 27. Letter to Arlene from Eleanor Burgess, St. Luke's Medical Center, Sioux City, Iowa:

> *We feel that you wish to have your transcript as soon as possible so are not delaying it by waiting for the fee but would appreciate your mailing the $2.00 at your earliest convenience.*

Arlene had been collecting transcripts and recommendations, and her papers were almost complete. The question was whether or not to trust the mail. As she was packing up during her final night in Kentucky, the phone rang. It was her good friend and fellow missionary nurse Mary Nell Harper on her way back to east Africa. She was in Hyden for a reunion of her own FNS graduating class. When the reunion wound down, Arlene drove across town to fetch Mary Nell and put her up for the night. The next morning, Arlene took the necessary Zambia registration forms to have them notarized. Then Mary Nell put the whole batch of papers into her carry-on luggage.

June 29. Arlene's cable to Sylvia Chesterman:

> *MEET MISS HARPER LUSAKA AIRPORT SUNDAY AFTERNOON JULY TWO FROM NAIROBI ENROUTE MALAWI CARRYING PACKAGE FOR YOU ARLENE SCHUITEMAN*

5

Spirit

Busiku ngunamasandu.
There are many changes that happen at night.

Up at 4:30 a.m. Today I left home after almost 1½ years at home on an extended furlough after being forced to leave beloved Ethiopia. Months of traumatic wounds of heart and spirit have now healed although the precious scars will always remain. God has graciously healed me and restored me. How I praise Him. He seemed to tarry but His timing is right. How marvelous are His ways.

August 19, 1978

Arlene dressed quickly. She had packed her flight bags the night before, and they were waiting by the door. Grada had heard the alarm and was standing in the kitchen in her robe—she hoped to get back to sleep because she had to go to work later. But she would not miss this goodbye for all the world. She had learned to brace herself for the momentousness of these post-furlough partings. When her sister first departed for Nasir in southern Sudan in 1955, Grada did not see her again for four years. As travel became easier, the world grew smaller, and time between family reunions grew shorter—either because Arlene came home sooner or her family visited her mission site.

But this morning was different; it felt like the most momentous leave-taking yet. Ma was failing, and she would never be able to visit

Arlene in Zambia. There was a strong possibility that she would be gone before Arlene returned home. One of these goodbyes would, indeed, be final.

During recent days, none of the three had spoken of this dark possibility that hung in the air, but Grada and Arlene both thought of it. They could only suppose that in her most lucid times, Ma had thought of it as well. And now the time for goodbyes was here.

Arlene washed her face and brushed her hair. She did not normally wear a lot of makeup, but there was no need for any today. She would end the day dozing on a plane. To be clean and comfortable was all that travel required, and Arlene was a long-distance traveling pro. She carried chewing gum, a small medical kit, her journal, a fine-point pen, and her smallest Bible.

She turned off the bathroom light and stepped across the hallway. Standing in the archway, she looked across the kitchen at Grada, who was leaning against the counter with her arms folded. Grada sighed.

"Should I—?" Arlene wondered aloud.

"You'd better."

"Will she even—?"

"If you don't, you won't forgive yourself."

"I can hear her sleeping so soundly."

Grada shrugged her shoulders. She was certainly not going to argue. "It's up to you."

Headlights flashed across the room as Shirley Meendering pulled her car into the driveway.

It was now or never.

Arlene eased open Ma's bedroom door. She crept carefully to the side of the bed and slowly lowered her hand onto her mother's shoulder. Startled, Ma's eyes popped open.

"It's Arlene, Ma."

Ma nodded.

"I'm leaving. I'm going to Africa."

Ma nodded. Arlene was not sure if her mother would remember this moment later. She glanced over her shoulder to make sure

Grada had followed her into the room. She had. Grada could tell Ma any part that needed reminding.

"I love you, Ma. I'll write often. I'll pray for you. I know you'll pray for me."

Ma nodded.

"I'll see you again, Ma. But not for a while."

Ma whispered something. Arlene knelt by the bed and put her head by her mother's mouth.

"What?"

"*Mijn lieve meisje* [My little sweetheart]."

Arlene swallowed hard. Now was not the time for tears; she did not want to upset her mother. But even if later in the day Ma forgot where Arlene had gone, at least for this moment she recognized who was kneeling by her bed, kissing her forehead, and whispering goodbye.

Shirley was a good friend of Arlene's. Like Arlene, she was single. She was also charismatic and had traveled with Arlene to the Kansas City ecumenical Conference on Charismatic Renewal the previous summer. You could say that Shirley was part of Arlene's inner circle. Arlene could let down her guard in that circle and talk about the gifts of the Holy Spirit at a time when American churches were splitting over the charismatic movement, especially as it related to worship styles. Arlene could not be at ease on these issues with all of her family members, so having a group of understanding and supportive friends was a balm for her.

Shirley was a faithful correspondent when Arlene was away from Sioux Center. When Shirley's health permitted, she joined the circle of prayer partners Arlene had established (Artella, Eunice, Frieda, Audrey, Marcia, and Joyce), a group that met weekly with Arlene when she was in town and continued praying for her when she was on the field. Shirley had been born with a serious heart murmur. Whereas surgeries during her youth had largely mitigated the issues, she remained careful, living with her parents at the farm where she was raised. This morning, when Grada needed to stay with Ma, Arlene could not have asked for a more empathetic companion as she wept her way to the Sioux City airport.

The plane lifted off the Iowa runway on schedule at 7:08 a.m. There was a long enough layover in Chicago for Arlene's youngest sister Milly to drive around the bottom of the lake from Michigan with Lee and the kids to have lunch with Aunt Arlene in the Windy City. That evening, the Lufthansa flight was packed full for the eighthour flight through the night to Frankfurt.

The sun was coming up in Germany when the plane landed. Breezy, a missionary friend, was there to meet Arlene. The two women drove thirty minutes south to the city of Darmstadt, which housed one of Arlene's favorite places on the planet: the Canaan retreat center. Arlene and Breezy arrived in time for Sunday morning Communion. They spent the next twenty-four hours conversing and praying with the Evangelical Sisters, several of whom were Arlene's dear friends. Like her inner circle back home and her beloved friends in Mettu, Arlene's spiritual practices were welcome here. The sisters were contemplative as well as charismatic in their spirituality. They embraced joyful worship, especially as it grew out of their leader Mother Basilea's teaching on the gift of daily repentance. Breezy and Arlene wandered about Canaan's spacious and serene grounds, talking about Ethiopia.

One of Arlene's special friends at Canaan was Sister Mechthild. Like Arlene, she lived her life in song. She was known to greet her friends singing and sing to them as they departed. Sister Mechthild met privately with Arlene to discuss where she was headed and why. When she learned Arlene would have a roommate at Katete, she counseled her, "Just remember the beam in your own eye and you won't see the splinter in hers." Arlene took the words not as a quaint biblical aphorism but—knowing Sister Mechthild's heart—as prophecy.

When Arlene and Leatta both agreed to teach at St. Francis, they were assigned to room together—but they were very different personalities. Leatta was both insecure and talkative, and so their relationship had the potential for difficulty. Arlene wrote Sister Mechthild's words in her journal and took them to heart. They would bear fruit, and her relationship with Leatta would become a great joy.

The Africa prayer group of Canaan met with Arlene and Breezy, who shared stories of the church in Ethiopia, and the Canaan group gave Arlene contacts in Zambia. That evening, it was time for Arlene to join the departure songs and return to the skies.

Back in Frankfurt, she made her way to the Kenya Airways ticket counter. Over the loudspeaker she heard the announcement for a flight to Addis Ababa. Later, she wrote in her journal,

Every cell in me longed for another night in Addis. I poured the desire out as a sacrifice.

Right on schedule, she boarded the flight for Nairobi, the capital city of Kenya.

The overnight flight to Africa took twelve hours, flying directly between her old homes—Nasir on the right and Mettu on the left. After she disembarked, she then had a six-hour wait in the Transient Lounge. She made her layover useful by telephoning a local pastor, who came to the airport to accept a package the sisters had asked Arlene to carry to him.

He informed her that Kenyan president Jomo Kenyatta had died that morning. Kenyatta had spent his life caring for his people, even changing his name to reference his nation. He had spent nine years in prison for his efforts promoting independence from Britain. Since Kenya's independence in 1963, Kenyatta had been considered the father of the nation. Arlene wondered how his death would impact stability in the region.

Her next flight was on Zambian Air, a three-hour flight further south. For the first time in her life, she would be living in the Southern Hemisphere. She landed in Lusaka about suppertime, although her body clock had no idea what time or day it really was. It was still morning in Sioux Center, seven hours earlier than the capital city of Zambia.

Arlene did not know what plans had been made for her arrival. The trip from Lusaka to Katete would be a walk of faith. But she was found easily by Philippa, the accountant of St. Francis Hospital. Philippa had the necessary employment permit, which Arlene wielded to navigate her way through customs. Using the hospital's truck, Philippa had driven to the city to pick up Arlene. They then went across town to their base, the Anglican mission, to get some rest and spend a few days shopping before the drive out to Katete. The next day, August 23, Arlene was able to buy her prescribed nursing uniforms and send a cable home:

HAPPY BIRTHDAY MOTHER EXCELLENT TRAVELS AS
SCHEDULED TO LUSAKA WILL PROCEED BY HOSPITAL
TRUCK TO KATETE SUNDAY LOVE ARLENE

On the Great East Road, the main highway from Zambia's centralized capital over to the Malawi border, Arlene noted how the landscape reminded her of the Sudan. The terrain along the highway was generally flat, but the rise and fall of small, distant hills gave the horizon layers of texture and color—though not as flat as southern Sudan or as hilly as Hyden, Kentucky. Although she arrived during the dry season, she spotted flowering vegetation along the way that included bougainvillea, poinsettia, hibiscus, and jacaranda. There were farms, but not set in rectangular borders like in Iowa. Just as the highway loped and curved, following the landscape, so did the farms. Wild grass—mostly brown this time of year—surrounded the farms of sandy soil.

The hospital truck was larger than a farm pickup truck and had beams of metal arching across its open back to support a tarp in the event of rain—though there was little chance of rain this time of year. Typical temperatures were 80 degrees Fahrenheit in the day and 55 at night. In a couple of months, daytime temperatures would climb to 100, and night would cool down quite a bit, but never enough to require central heating.

The route the women took across the eastern half of Zambia started at 4,200 feet above sea level, wound its way 3,000 feet down into the Luangwa River Valley, and then climbed back up to 3,500 feet at Katete.

When the truck pulled onto the grounds at St. Francis Hospital, Leatta came running to welcome the weary traveler to her new home. Arlene had been living out of her suitcase for nine days, and she soon discovered she would be living out of it for many more weeks. A new apartment was being prepared for Arlene and Leatta, but they were told it would not be ready for six weeks. That prediction fell short by a few months.

The travelers had arrived in time for the 3:00 p.m. Sunday service at the Reformed Church, which was started by Dutch missionaries who had come north from South Africa. Arlene was eager to attend. That day's attendance, including the new tutor, was typical: twenty-two women, twenty-two children, and three men.

During her orientation over the next few days, Arlene learned that the hospital had 315 beds. The pattern for the wards was to place sixty wrought-iron beds together in one large room with enough space between patients for a nurse or doctor to squeeze in sideways. Arlene had an office at the nursing school, which she immediately diagnosed as filthy and unorganized. Fine dust and sand covered every surface. No worries. If there was one thing Arlene knew how to do, it was clean.

Of much greater concern was the state of the mission itself. The site's founding visionary was Father Francis Trefusis, a priest who believed that caring for the body was a precursor to caring for the spirit. His vision in founding St. Francis was to create a teaching hospital where students would follow in the footsteps of Francis of Assisi, the twelfth-century mystic who saw in every sick person the face of Jesus. Father Trefusis had high hopes for this institution:

> In this hospital I hope we shall try not only to follow in the footsteps of St. Francis, but also to train medical orderlies, infused, as much as in us lies, with His Spirit. Pray God it may come true.

Arlene could quickly see that Trefusis's vision was all but lost. The staff and students were no longer encouraged to take any interest either in the namesake of the place or in the religion that named him a saint.

On Monday, August 28, the day after arriving at Katete, Arlene was up at 6:00 a.m. Leatta accepted Arlene's invitation to pray together. Then Arlene walked over to the school and gave her first anatomy lecture to the fourteen students—who were starting nursing school that day with a new tutor.

Back in Iowa, her supporting churches posted on their bulletin boards the form letter Arlene had placed in the mail a week before departure. At the end of the letter, she typed this verse:

> *Not by might, nor by power, but by my Spirit, says the Lord of Hosts—you will succeed because of my Spirit, though you are few and weak. Zechariah 4:6b* [TLB]

6

Time

Lingu-lingu kumuunda muchaamba tamulingulwi.
One can check what is going on in the fields but you
cannot check what is going on in somebody's heart.

---

*I hope we can arrange days so that Sat p.m. is not so
busy. No time to visit people at all. School and house
work takes up all our time. House hasn't been dusted
properly for 2 weeks. To bed at 9:30.*

September 9, 1978

Her first week at Katete felt like a month. She tried to rise by 5:00
a.m. each day to pursue her usual morning routine as best as she
could. Her classes began at 7:00 a.m., and she lectured for five hours
of the day. She often attended the training sessions that resident
doctors and clinical nursing instructors gave to her students. The
remaining hours were filled with Education Committee meetings
(of which she was the chair), Disciplinary Committee meetings, staff
meetings, the writing of quizzes and exams, the grading of quizzes
and exams, individual student conferences, official correspondence,
and interviews with prospective students.

Although the school would naturally undergo a transition under
new leadership, Arlene determined not to make any major changes
until the senior students finished their final course sequences and
graduated. Then she would consider adjustments. For now, her goal
was to clean the offices and attend to the filing tasks that, she and
Leatta agreed, were unacceptably in arears.

These tasks often kept Arlene at school until 7:00 p.m. She assumed it was just the first week, then just the first month, and then just the first term. Then she stopped assuming. The system was broken. She could not accomplish all that was expected of her. Neither could Leatta. They were good teachers and they worked hard. But the school was short-staffed with no hope of change on the horizon.

Compounding the problem was that the school was not the sum of their responsibilities. Arlene and Leatta had housecleaning, laundry, grocery shopping, and cooking. Cooking came with extra challenges. The water needed to be boiled before drinking and allowed to settle before they could use it for cooking or even cleaning. The electricity went off early each night and sometimes disappeared during the daytime. One day, shortly after they had purchased a few pounds of beef, the electricity died. With no refrigeration, Leatta set about cooking all the meat they had so it would not spoil. But that was not enough, because without the cool air, tiny ants attacked the cooked meat, even inside the refrigerator. They needed to rethink food management. They gravitated to cooking one chicken a week and then parsing it out into an entrée, a casserole, sandwiches, salads, and soup.

Then there was correspondence. The mail delivery was erratic, but when it arrived, it was a blizzard. That was a thrill to see, but it was a challenge to even read the mail let alone reply to all of it.

Arlene also needed to nurture her spirit. She read her Bible, prayed, and wrote in her journal every day. She usually listened to a Christian speaker on cassette tape, since she did not often hear a sermon in English during weekend worship. She did attend worship, three times every Sunday: 6:30 a.m. for Communion liturgy at the Anglican chapel, 3:00 p.m. for the Reformed Church worship service, and 7:00 p.m. for evensong back at the chapel. The Reformed service was in Nyanja. The services that bookended the day were spoken in the majestic language of the Book of Common Prayer, led by Father Hewitt, who was eighty-eight when Arlene first met him. Those services had only a handful in attendance and seldom included anything other than what the prayer book dictated.

Leatta was glad to pray with Arlene in the evenings at their home, but there was a slight danger that praying might lead to talking, and neither of them had time left over for conversation—there was the necessity of sleep. Arlene tried to lie down by 9:00 each night, hoping she could drift off in spite of the multiple threats of heat, army ants, mosquitos, rodents, roaches, lizards, and the occasional snake. She was not new to rural east Africa, but living there still required a period of adjustment after a time away.

Every staff member at the hospital had a car, with the exception of Arlene and Leatta. Others could go shopping or out to see the neighborhood without having to arrange transportation. If they had a few minutes of break, they could dash the six miles downtown to the post office to see if the mail had arrived. They could hope someday to travel the width and breadth of this glorious country, seeing its animals and geographical splendor. They could even visit *Mosi-oa-Tunya*, one of the largest waterfalls in the world. But not yet.

Arlene and Leatta began to feel trapped.

It wasn't as though they didn't have support. James and Faith Cairns, the administrators at St. Francis, were helpful and kind. They invited the new tutors to tea, but other than that, they tried to stay out of their way. They knew how busy their jobs must be, especially in the first year. They told Arlene the rules, set up weekly meetings, and then stepped aside.

Arlene recognized that life was intense for the nursing students as well. Students were organized in "Sets," with a new Set of about twenty students added every six months. A Set graduated every two years, which meant that four Sets were matriculating through at any given time. The Set that started at the same time as Arlene and Leatta was "Set 54," indicating that the school was twenty-seven years old. The Sets alternated their classroom work with hands-on education in the hospital wards. Each Set would circulate into the classroom for a week at a time and then return to ward work. Arlene calculated that during their two years of nurses training, the students spent only twelve weeks in class. During their remaining eight-four weeks, they functioned as unpaid labor for the hospital. Being the only hospital in that region of 100,000 people, the hospital relied on the help of those student nurses, and the students learned a great deal through on-the-job training.

The school never stopped, because there were always patients to care for. Even national holidays were school days at St. Francis. Although there were no classes on Saturdays, they were exam days. The pace was unrelenting.

Arlene plodded forward. She told herself and also her supporters that she loved teaching in Africa, even though it was sometimes difficult. She refused to let herself succumb to bitterness or ingratitude, but keeping a positive attitude wasn't always easy. One month after arriving at Katete, she wrote in her journal before walking over to the school to administer an exam:

Saturday. Up at 5:30. Cairns just leaving for the game park. Forgive me, God, for complaining about

> *—the tiny ants on everything*
> *—the dirty water*
> *—the lack of electricity*
> *—the long working days*

I am seeing now how awful murmuring and negativism is and how it must grieve you. Thank you for bringing me here and opening my eyes to it. Please infuse me with your strength to dispel the deep tiredness I feel this morning.

Arlene's personal, professional, and spiritual practices were mostly effective at keeping her life on an even keel. But additional factors impacted Arlene's journey through the autumn of 1978. Two days after writing that prayer in her journal, she opened a letter from her sister Bernice that told her Ma had fallen over sitting in a lawn chair and broken her arm, necessitating two nights in the hospital. Arlene was devastated that she was not the nurse on duty. Later that day, she had to tell two students that they were failing. They immediately resigned from the program, saying they would find another nursing school to attend.

Soon after, Leatta stepped into Arlene's office. "I was walking past the dorm and Mrs. Mzamo, the dorm mother, waved me over. She took me into her apartment and shut the door. She says, 'The students think I don't have ears, Sister Leatta.' Here we go, I think."

"Oh boy," said Arlene. "What?"

"Mrs. Mzamo said the girls that are failing were complaining."

"To Mrs. Mzamo?"

"No, to some of the other girls that Mrs. Mzamo was overhearing."

"Should I even be listening to this?"

"No, but just this one thing. The other girls said to them—"

"Said to who?"

"To the girls that are failing—they told those girls that the reason they're failing is that the new tutors have too high standards. They told them they should be allowed to pass if they have 45 percent, not 70 percent! I asked Mrs. Mzamo, 'Who was telling them that they can pass with 45 percent?' And Mrs. Mzamo says she'd rather not gossip, but if it was up to her, the students who said that should be failing too."

Arlene smiled. "Good for you, Alice Mzamo."

Leatta went on, "I asked her to tell me who should be failing so I could check their grades, and she said she didn't want to get in the middle of it—but, and this is why I'm telling you all this—she said that one of the students was thinking of starting a petition drive against the new tutors."

Arlene sat back and folded her arms.

"Mrs. Mzamo said to tell Sister Arlene to be ready."

"Leatta . . . do you think our standards are too high?"

"Forty-five percent? Ha! Never heard of such a thing!"

Arlene nodded. "Right. But this is not about grades . . . or the emotions of juveniles. It's about the Father of Lies and Darkness. We need to pray."

"Absolutely, Arlene."

Between being overwhelmed, feeling isolated, and quashing a student coup, what else could go wrong for Arlene and Leatta? More. Much more. Two weeks later, the military would be on high alert, and for a time, no one was allowed westward on the Great East Road.

7

Josh

Wako nabisya mbuchi.
Even if your child commits an offense,
you still like him.

Went with Hanneke and Winnie to Chipata. Enquiring about Driver's License and at customs about importing a new car. A new Renault 4 is $4000 and would require 150% customs. Outrageous. A used car at $2000 is 75%. God help me to do the right thing. It was 6 weeks since I had been off this place or even sat in a car.

October 19, 1978

Arlene caught a ride with two of her St. Francis colleagues into Chipata, the administrative center of Eastern Province. She was desperately low on groceries and supplies, and she decided to take in hand her need for transportation independence. Chipata was only fifty-five miles by car from the hospital, so a shopping trip could be accomplished in an afternoon if one was traveling by car. Catching the bus on the Great East Road was also possible, but the buses were not always running these days, and one might get into Chipata and not be able to get back.

Arlene had been told that passing the Zambian driver's examination was difficult. But she thought she had better start studying, even though she did not yet have a car. She collected the necessary information in Chipata and set to work. The day after she obtained her driving book and was preparing to become a licensed Zambian driver, word came that war had erupted in central Zambia. Arlene wrote in her journal:

200 dead—600 wounded.

Rhodesia (now known as Zimbabwe) to Zambia's south was struggling for independence, and in an age of jet planes and long-range artillery, a complex military strife spilled over the border. Zambia's President Kaunda warned his nation, "I want all of you to brace for a long war." Arlene's plans for travel were about to be threatened.

The U.S. Embassy sent word that Americans, like the two new tutors at the Nurses Training School of St. Francis, should be ready to leave at a moment's notice. Arlene rolled her eyes at the embassy warning. She had heard many such warnings during her years on the African continent. Besides, she was still essentially living out of her suitcase in temporary housing. This is Africa, she thought; things will change. She went about her business and continued to study for her driving test.

Dr. Cairns said that everyone should avoid the Great East Road for now. No trips west toward Lusaka were prudent, but hesitant travel east to Chipata was still possible.

"Arlene, there's news. Well, bad news for us but perhaps good news for you." Faith Cairns had stopped by the school looking for the principal tutor.

"Hello, Mrs. Cairns," Arlene said. "I'm sorry about your bad news. What's happened?"

"Dr. Thomas has announced his departure."

"Oh dear. We're all going to miss him. Where will he go?"

"Where the money is, I suppose. That's the place we lose most of our doctors to. But this is the news for you: he has a swell car. I told him not to send the word around till I could speak with you first. I know you've been inquiring, and I wanted to see if you'd like to bag it right off."

"It's the blue one?"

"Right. A Datsun, I believe. Never a breakdown, says he. He is asking 3,000 kwacha, which is a lot, but reasonable given the market."

Arlene shook her head. "That's nearly 4,000 U.S. dollars—same as a brand-new car."

"But you need to recall the whale of a customs fee for bringing one in. This one's here, and you save a bundle on a private sale."

"Well, it is something I'm praying about. I should speak with him."

"Indeed. But don't wait long, dear."

Two days later, Arlene borrowed the Datsun to drive over to town, hoping to avoid the police. It was her first attempt at driving while sitting on the right. Worse was driving on the left side of the road, which made her feel certain she was bound for a head-on collision. That experience was, well, an experience, but she knew she would have to get used to this holdover from British culture.

Dr. Thomas was waiting for her when she returned. "What do you think of it?

"It handles well. As good as I'm capable of anyway."

"It's the 1200 model. It has never had a breakdown. We would love to take her along, but there are the port fees we already paid once, so it is best if she stays. We will sell her to the first buyer."

Arlene smiled, but instead of commenting on his logic, she asked, "How many miles per gallon? I'm sorry—kilometers per liter?"

"Fourteen. That is very good. The advantages of a compact car."

"I'll have to pass the driver's exam."

Dr. Thomas moved hurriedly on, since he did not want to make the sale contingent on Arlene's negotiations with the Road Transport and Safety Agency. "I have collected a number of spare parts. I will give you those for no additional—"

Arlene continued thinking aloud. "I've always driven on the right side of the road."

"It has a steering wheel lock and also a key for the petrol cap. It is very difficult to steal this car."

"Leatta and I would very much like to go see Victoria Falls."

"The 'Smoke That Thunders'! That is a requirement! One of the seven natural wonders of the world. When you drive toward it, you can see the spray from forty kilometers away. This car has been there many times. You will not have to steer—the car knows the way. What do you think?"

"I think I would like to say—"

"Wait. Before you speak, there is one thing more. There is a little dog named Josh. He will not like India; he insists on staying with the car. So, I must speak for him and tell you that without him, you cannot buy the car."

Arlene was quite surprised by this development. She did not need the extra burden of a pet. But given the amount of burglary here, a guard dog in the yard might come in handy.

Dr. Thomas volunteered, "I can lower the kwacha to 2,750. What do you say?"

Arlene held out her hand, and Dr. Thomas shook it. She was the proud owner of an eight-year-old blue Datsun with 52,000 miles—plus a small, black and tan German shepherd mixed-breed named after an Old Testament warrior.

Over the next month, Arlene crammed every spare minute with memorizing the driver's manual. On December 19, Dr. Thomas set the whole day aside to accompany her into Chipata. They presented the car itself for a road worthiness test, which it passed. She purchased insurance and transferred the title and license plate to her name. Then after stopping by the bank and the post office, they had lunch at the Coffee Pot.

The last stop of the day was the R.T.S.A., the driver's license office. This part of the Zambian Driver's License exam was oral rather than written. She had to identify traffic signs by shape, color, and purpose, and they asked her to recite from memory the ten basic rules of driving. She was given driving situations and asked how she should respond. Finally, she drove through the traffic cones with an instructor on her left. She passed, whispering, "Thank you, dear Jesus!"

Back in Katete, Dr. Thomas handed Arlene the keys and Josh's food dish. Both the car and the dog were hers. On January 3, Arlene's fifty-fifth birthday, the two American tutors finally took a drive into Chipata on their own. They stopped by the post office, and lo and behold, Arlene's air freight had finally arrived from the United States after five months in transit. There was a bit of damage to the carton, and a few items had either fallen out or been stolen. Still, it felt so good to have this connection to her old life; and just in time, because the next day they received the keys to their new home and could finally move in. At last, Zambia was starting to feel like home.

Over the next year, military flare-ups became fewer, and Rhodesia formally became Zimbabwe in 1980. That spring, Arlene and Leatta drove the Datsun west of Lusaka for the first time, following the Line of Rail toward Livingstone. By now, they had been colleagues at St. Francis for a year and a half. They had become much more than colleagues—they were good friends with respect and trust for each other. Arlene found in Leatta a disciplined and energetic worker. She had a simple, almost austere lifestyle, and when Arlene learned that Leatta was sending every extra cent home for her mother's care, she admired her all the more.

Before going to the falls, the two nurses wanted to visit another mission station and nursing school—the very one Arlene had applied to first: Macha. So, they turned north at Choma and followed a forty-mile, dusty, washboard road to the Macha Mission Hospital compound. They stayed there for two nights, receiving an excellent tour of the hospital and the Zambia Enrolled Nurses School. Arlene noted the beauty of the grounds and the warmth of the staff she met. She felt a tinge of jealousy but pushed it down, trusting that God had placed her at Katete.

The next day, Arlene and Leatta rose with the sun to get on the road as soon as it was safe. (Night travel in the African bush was not a good idea for a multitude of reasons.) They backtracked on the washboard to Choma, and then turned southwest for three more hours before seeing in the distance their first glimpse of mist from the falls.

Mosi-oa-Tunya turned out to be everything they had expected: it was spectacular. There were actually four separate falls with an average drop of 326 feet. They took in the view from both sides of the border, walking across to Zimbabwe. At the museum, they saw the original coat, cap, and traveling case of missionary and explorer Dr. David Livingstone, who gave the falls its British name and for whom the town was named. The artifacts, the namesake town, and the statue of the man all placed this missionary on a pedestal—something Arlene thought should never be done. She was grateful for the history lesson as far as it went, but she was ready to head back to work.

Josh transitioned easily to his new owner, and he already knew the hospital and the staff. He was a small, scrappy dog used to running free and investigating the neighborhood. The hospital grounds were away from town and ungated. There were several dogs there—all country dogs, not city dogs—and they were valued for the ways they protected the area. Josh's food dish was placed in a new yard, but that was no problem for him as long as it was filled each day. He came to recognize Arlene's call and learned that Arlene's yard was now his yard and therefore his responsibility. He would not accept any animal or human thievery happening on his watch, and he sounded an alarm to let everyone know he was on guard. Arlene was comforted rather than bothered by his warnings. He soon became more than a protector to Arlene. He was a loyal friend, and she loved him.

Three years into her time in Zambia, Arlene would move across the country to a new post. Though Josh went with her, that transition turned out to be a devastating one for him. The trauma started with getting him into the car. He was not used to riding in vehicles. He had seldom been off the hospital grounds except on his own four feet. For the first two hours of the trip, he was barking and shaking. At the new hospital, the local dogs did not accept him. He would not bow to them, but some of them were far better fighters and Josh was often bitten and bloodied. He learned to stay close to Arlene and follow her to the nursing school, the hospital, and even church. He would sit close to whatever building she was in and accompany her home. When she had to go north for General Nursing Council meetings, Josh would chase the car until his pads were injured. Then he would limp home. But he would never allow himself to be chained.

Arlene was a farmer's daughter. Her parents would never allow animals in the house. They also taught their girls that part of caring for animals included making the difficult decision of when to "put them down." From Arlene's perspective, Josh's life had become miserable.

One afternoon, during a Hospital Management Board meeting, a staff member complained about the growing number of dogs on the place. He said that he and his wife were having difficulty sleeping because of the barking. Arlene knew that Josh was one of the contributors. She also knew that her precious dog was scratched up or bit up or torn up all the time. Her farmer's-daughter-self rose within her. She pulled one of the doctors aside after the meeting and asked for some phenobarbital—enough to put a dog to sleep. That night, Josh got a steak for supper.

The next day was May 1, Zambia's Labor Day, and her new school had the day off. Arlene wrote in her journal:

A traumatic day for me. God gave me a faithful watchdog and friend, and it <u>hurt</u> to put him to sleep. God, I ask Your guardian angels to protect from thieves and burglars. Heal the hurt I feel today. It's good it was a holiday.

8

Medicine

Atika maanzi aatakwe buyoleke.
Once water spills, you cannot gather it again.

---

*News that an unlabeled bottle of medicine
"chloroquine" was given in a village and some 26
children have died! Bodies sent to Chipata for
examination.*

March 16, 1979

When Arlene arrived at Katete, she was working with someone else's standards. All four current Sets of student nurses had been interviewed and admitted by someone else. Apparently, prior to Arlene's teaching, some of those students had earned less than 50 percent on their coursework and were, nonetheless, hoping to pass their final exams (administered by the General Nursing Council).

The new principal tutor's assessment was that the situation was grim. Arlene saw students who should never have been admitted, and she saw students who should not continue. She even saw nurses now graduated and working at the hospital who should not have been certified and allowed to care for patients.

Arlene was a missionary called to respect the culture of which she was a guest. Her task was not to make wholesale changes to the local culture; instead, she labored alongside her new friends, colleagues, and patients to seek what was most truthful, beautiful, and helpful. But when Arlene looked at the St. Francis culture, she said, "Not good enough." Although she knew she could not do perfectly, she knew could certainly do better—with God's help of course. She wrote to her prayer circle back in Sioux Center:

> *We are trying to raise the standard of nursing care, but it is a slow process. We really need more clinical instructors for closer supervision. We will keep working on it.*

The standards were too low, the staff too meager, the schedule too overwhelming, and the school's vision obscured. It was time to roll up her sleeves.

Zambia, both at St. Francis and beyond its doors, was a confluence of cultures—ancient and modern, tribal and democratic, superstitious and scientific. Medical care in the African bush was a hodgepodge of folk medicine and contemporary therapies and pharmaceuticals.

Arlene's profession brought her face-to-face with great pain. She witnessed realities that caused her to ask "Why?" and say "If only." Since some of this suffering was preventable, she was astonished at what brought patients to the hospital in the first place. Especially heartbreaking were the burn patients. Some of these patients were epileptics, who had fallen into a fire and ended up with serious burns. Such incidents were predictable, given that most meals in rural households were cooked on open fires rather than stoves. The common belief in rural Zambian culture was that during an epileptic seizure, observers must be careful not to touch the patient. If they did, the illness could spread to them. This myth created the following precept: If someone falls into a fire, you cannot be sure why; therefore, it is safest to stand back.

Arlene wondered how such a belief system arose. Was it passed down from generation to generation? Or did it emanate from traditional medicine men and women? Arlene knew such a man at the open-air Katete market. He had nailed a sign to a tree that read "The African Doctor," and he had spread his medicines and magic charms on low tables in front of him. He attracted a crowd of customers, and Arlene wanted to stop each one of them and ask on what basis they trusted this man. She certainly did not trust him. She had a history of medical and spiritual conflict with such "doctors" that went all the way back to her days at Nasir. She thought she might someday forget herself and flip the tables of "The African Doctor" like Jesus and the moneychangers.

When, she wondered, does cultural respect become enablement of nonsense?

She longed for better medicine for her students and their patients. Of course, her theology denied her a perfect world. The world, she believed, would become perfect only with the return of Jesus. Until then, her task was to work and pray that God's will would be done "on earth as it is in heaven." Such was the tension with which she lived. Her struggle with the Zambian students, patients, and culture was what it meant for her to take up her cross and follow Christ.

Sometimes St. Francis itself was the source of harm. In the spring of 1979, the hospital's pharmacist and one of the doctors both contracted serious tropical illnesses. The pharmacist was diagnosed with hepatitis and laid low for about three months. Someone took over his job at the hospital and prepared a bottle of chloroquine, intended as a malaria medication, to be sent to a dresser in a nearby village. The mixture in the bottle was adult strength, but the dresser distributed it to a group of children, giving them all an overdose. It was rumored back at St. Francis that as many as twenty-six children had died as a result. The police came to the hospital, and Dr. Cairns made a sudden trip to Lusaka. All was hush-hush. A chemical intended to heal turned out to be worse than the potions at the foot of the tree of "The African Doctor."

The St. Francis doctor with the tropical illness was taken by stretcher to the Chipata airport and flown to London where, not long after, he succumbed to the disease. He had come to St. Francis to bring healing, but his service had brought about his own demise. The British doctor had tried to do some good and thereby walked into harm's way. That was the struggle he, Arlene, and all the medical professionals and future medical professionals at St. Francis faced every day.

9

Chickens

Luuwo luza atunji.
Wind comes with a lot of things.

Charles Mumba from ZNS came to pick up pkg of N.T. this evening and he gave a great testimony of the Lord's work in their camp near Katete. One boy possessed by 10 demons was delivered of them all. We've asked him to come for an NCF mtg.

June 22, 1979

"Sister Schuiteman, I need to miss classes tomorrow." One of the nursing students had been waiting for the other students to leave the classroom.

"Why? What's happening, Edina?"

"My grandfather wants me to bring a chicken to the cemetery."

"Is there a funeral?"

Edina shook her head.

"Have you told him that you can't bring him a chicken because you're in nursing school?"

"I can't do that."

"Why can't you?"

"He's dead."

This was a new one. Arlene probed further. "I'm sorry, I don't understand."

"He died last year. And now his spirit bothers me all the time."

Now it was becoming clear. Arlene had witnessed many exorcisms during her time in Ethiopia, and she acknowledged the dangerous influence of spirits. "How does his spirit bother you?"

"In my dreams. I cannot get good sleep. He tells me things I have to do for him. He says he will make things worse if I do not. I have to do them. So tomorrow I have to miss class and take a chicken to his grave."

"What can he do to you, Edina? How can he make things worse?"

Edina looked panicked. "I don't want to find out. Please do not make me find out."

Arlene came to her side. "Edina, have you attended Nurses Christian Fellowship?"

"No."

"All right. I'll make you a bargain. I will let you miss class tomorrow if you will attend Nurses Christian Fellowship sometime."

"I can do that."

"Thank you. But get the notes. You'll still have to take the quiz."

"Yes, Sister. Thank you."

At her church in Mettu, Ethiopia, Arlene had been a support person during exorcisms. She provided prayer, compassion, and medical care when needed, but she herself did not command the demons to depart. In other words, she played the role of a nurse rather than a surgeon. Now in Zambia, she felt that surely there must be evil spirits at work in her neighborhood, as evidenced by ancestor worship and some disturbing traditional medicine practices. She saw little evidence that the now eighty-nine-year-old Father Hewitt at the Anglican chapel would know what to do at an exorcism. So she prayed that God would send help.

At the same time, something similarly ominous was looming thirty miles up the road from St. Francis, which Arlene wouldn't find out until later when Charles Mumba, a young soldier stationed at the Zambian National Service (ZNS) camp, would visit her. Being a Christian, where he started a Bible study with a few other young soldiers in ZNS who were also fulfilling their national responsibility at that base in the Eastern Province.

One night during Bible study, a young man—a boy really—attended the meeting. As Charles spoke, the boy suddenly fell to the ground and cried out in anguish. No one there knew what to do. Charles had never experienced anything like this episode before. "Who are you?" Charles asked the boy.

Instead of the boy's voice, growls emerged and he shouted, "I am the devil!"

Being familiar with the Gospel story of the Gerasene man possessed by many demons, Charles asked, "How many are you?"

"Ten!"

"How did you enter this boy?" Charles had the boldness to ask.

"We entered when he was empty."

Charles turned to the other soldiers and commanded, "Pray! Ask the Lord to protect you so when the spirits leave this boy, they will not enter any of us." Then he turned back to the boy and, using the same words as the apostle Paul in the book of Acts, proclaimed, "In the name of Jesus Christ, I command you to come out of him!"

The boy thrashed and wept, and a voice cried, "I am going!" and the boy lay still.

Charles touched the boy. "Are you all right?"

The boy began to thrash and cry out again, "I am the devil!" Charles repeated his command, and a voice once again said, "I am going!" This exchange was repeated nine times. On the tenth time, the boy convulsed harder than ever, and the voice said, "I am taking this boy with me into the wilderness!"

"No! You cannot have this boy! In the name of Jesus of Nazareth, the crucified and risen Lord, the Christ, the finder of lost sheep, and the guardian of this child, I insist that you must leave. Go!"

"I am going," it said, and the room fell silent. The boy lay still. Charles laid his hand on the boy's shoulder, and the boy opened his eyes.

"What happened?" he asked. Only later would he learn the details of the great struggle that had occurred.

Near the end of that month, Charles appeared in Arlene's office doorway in his military fatigues. "Are you Sister Schuiteman?"

"Hello. Yes, I am. Who are you?"

"I'm Charles Mumba, ma'am. I'm from the ZNS camp. I've been told you have a supply of New Testaments you're willing to share."

"Oh yes, of course. I have them from the Gideons. How many would you like?"

"Well, I don't know. Things are changing fast." He went on to tell her about the Bible study, the incident with the ten demons, and the numbers of soldiers accepting Christ after witnessing the change in the delivered boy.

Having seen such events in Ethiopia, Arlene got an idea. "Charles, may I ask a request of you?"

"*Mwamtheradi* [Absolutely]."

"We have a group called Nurses Christian Fellowship. About thirty nursing students attend on Tuesday evenings. It was started long ago, and by the time I came here, it was more social than spiritual. I'm trying to change that focus, bit by bit. I'd love it if you would come back here on a Tuesday and share your testimony."

Charles stepped further into the room. "Do you believe a person can be saved?"

"With all my heart."

"May I ask your nurses if they want to be saved?"

Arlene nodded, guessing that he was the answer to her prayer. "Please ask them that, Charles. Please."

The following Tuesday, a phone message was left at the hospital switchboard. Charles Mumba was asking if someone could come and pick him up along the Great East Road at the turnoff to the ZNS camp. Leatta and Arlene jumped into the Datsun and drove thirty miles to get him and thirty miles back. They made it back in time to feed Charles supper before NCF.

The room was full. Charles told his dramatic story and then asked, "Do you want to be saved?" No one moved. Charles told them he would stay at St. Francis until Friday, if anyone wanted to come and speak with him.

Many of the nurses visited with Charles the next day. Arlene couldn't tell if their interest was spiritual or simply the desire to spend time with a kind, young man on a mostly female campus. That afternoon and evening, Charles spoke with three different groups on the hospital grounds. As Arlene and Leatta fed Charles a late supper, they learned that a few of the nurses had responded and prayed to give their hearts to Christ.

On Charles's last day, Arlene asked Edina if she would go and speak with him.

"Why do you want me to see him?" Edina asked.

"I want you to tell him about your grandfather."

"My grandfather doesn't like me talking about him."

"What grandfather wouldn't love to have his granddaughter talk about him?"

"You don't know my grandfather."

"Actually, I might," said Arlene. "I'll go with you to see Charles."

Edina spoke with Charles in the yard outside the school. She told him that the spirit of her grandfather had been bothering her sleep and demanding her to do things for him.

"I'm going to speak to you," Charles responded, "but I don't want you to answer, Edina. I'll be speaking to someone else." Then he said, "In the name of Jesus Christ, tell me who you are who is troubling this girl."

Edina closed her eyes and screamed. Arlene leapt to her side, praying. Edina cried out, "I am devil!" and then again, in another voice, "I am evil!" As a crowd of student nurses watched, Charles commanded, "I am a servant of Jesus, and I tell you both that you must leave her and never return!"

Later that evening, Arlene wrote in her journal:

Edina Moyo delivered of 2 demons today by the authority of Jesus the Son of God. Many came to witness it. God, bless those who gave their hearts to you today and yesterday. This is a beginning for them. For this place.

The next morning, Arlene drove Charles into town to the bus station. In a letter to her circle of praying friends, she invited them to petition against the spiritual opposition she expected now that they had stepped across into enemy territory.

On July 11, the space station Skylab fell from the sky like lightening, scattering debris across western Australia. The next morning, Arlene started a three-day fast, a practice she had developed in Ethiopia. In spite of her lack of energy and time, she decided to start a Bible study. She stopped attending evensong and told her students she would be leading weekly Bible classes at her home. By that fall, there were seven nurses studying the book of Genesis in Arlene's living room on Sunday evenings.

A few days after Arlene started the Bible study, she was appointed to the General Nursing Council (GNC) of Zambia. Although she didn't know how she would fulfill that responsibility without additional staff, she also felt she couldn't turn down the opportunity to improve the quality of nursing in Zambia.

At the start of her first three-year term on the GNC, she attended meetings at Kabwe, where she worshipped at the United Church of Zambia. Pastor Rev. Sinyangwe showed her true Zambian hospitality by driving her to see the railroads, the mines, the hospital, and the overall town. Before returning her to the GNC meeting, he wanted to give her a gift, so they stopped by his house. There he presented her with a bag of mangos, a box of cookies, and one live chicken. The gift of a chicken was a common gesture of respect and hospitality in this culture. This caught Arlene off guard. But she didn't want to offend the reverend, so she accepted his gifts.

He smiled and said, "Do not worry. Give the chicken to the chef where you are staying. He will know what to do." Sure enough, the chef prepared the fowl for supper that night, complete with stuffing.

10

Daughter

Kukobboka kwanzila nkukwichindiila.
A path becomes a path if one frequently uses it.

Up at 4:15. To Lilongwe. Stayed at Hotel. Hair cut at Tiffany. Grocery shopping. Very nice day. Glasses frame broke.

> *August 11, 1979*

Phoned home at 6 a.m. talked to Grada. Very nice. $15.60. To Presby Church. Riding around new city. Home at 4 p.m.

> *August 12, 1979*

For her mother's eighty-second birthday, Arlene decided to give her the gift of a telephone call. Such a gift would require a four-hour drive to the capital city of Malawi. The price of the telephone call itself would be about ten dollars per minute, but it would be worth it. Timing would be difficult given Arlene's busy class schedule combined with the time difference. Arlene did call, but she had miscalculated the time difference, and Ma was in bed sound asleep. Arlene spoke briefly with Grada, which was grand.

After her return to Katete, the daughter sat down to send her mother a birthday card, well aware the card would be late, if it arrived at all. The card had a painting of pink and purple pansies on the front with a Bible verse inside:

Faith is the substance of things hoped for,
the evidence of things not seen. (Hebrews 11:1)

Arlene wrote her birthday greeting in cursive, rather than the tiny block print she typically used in her journal entries. She filled the letter with details designed to allow Ma into the mundane moments of her Zambian life but also to evoke memories, especially those to which an Iowa farm wife could relate. Those images of time past were a gift to Johanna Rozeboom Schuiteman and also an enchanting record for future generations.

> *Katete*
> *19 August 1979*

Dear Ma:

> *It is a year ago today that I left home to go to Zambia. You were sleeping at 4:30 a.m. when I woke you to say good-bye. I wonder if you still remember that. It would be nice if I could come to say Happy Birthday but that can't be possible this year. Even this card will come too late, but I hope you remember that I phoned last week after you were in bed already, and Grada was in the basement taking a shower. Did she tell you that I called for your birthday?*

> *Two years ago all of us were home at the same time to celebrate your birthday. We celebrated in an Orange City restaurant. That was your 80th.*

> *Yesterday I baked bread but it isn't as good as you used to make. I also made rhubarb sauce. I canned five pints. We use all our glass jars as soon as they are empty and now have less than two dozen saved up from coffee jars, peanut butter, and jam. I also canned 2 jars of tomatoes. Now all the jars are full. But the garden is resting too until the rains come. It takes too much water to water everything by hand. We've been eating strawberries for a week now—real nice ones.*

> *Do you still remember how you used to tell us not to ride with strangers and then when your cousin, Gerrit Franken, wanted to*

give us a ride we refused? Then when we got home, there he was visiting at our house!

Sometimes we would come home and we smelled Grandpa Schuiteman's cigars, and Grandma had a purse, a black velvet one, and always peppermints in it. I remember when Grandpa Rozeboom would come when we were sick, and he would bring his thermometer to take our temperature—and pray for us.

I also remember all the clothes hanging in the house to dry in the winter time—and Pa's underwear hanging on a coat hanger. Do you still remember that? And Grada always said killowpace instead of pillow case, and canpake instead of pancake?

I did my washing and ironing yesterday—washing by hand— that's quite a job with big sheets and Turkish towels. And ironing on the workbench, especially white cotton uniforms—but "it stick niet so krec."

I'm wearing my old glasses since the other frame broke. I wonder if Bob Vermeer sent a new pair for me already. I think a stronger glass case would be better. It must have happened when I had them in my purse and was carrying boxes, etc.

This week 25 new students are coming. One sent a telegram yesterday and said her father had died and she would be late in coming.

The next 6-7 weeks will be extra busy.

I have some calla lilies in the house. My geraniums look real nice—and also red salvia. We water them and also the little fruit trees. It is very dry. How is the summer weather there? Is it hot enough to use the air conditioner?

Well, it's dinner time so I will stop. We are having chicken.

Love,
Arlene

11

Matthew

Kupa nkwanzika.
Giving is reserving for future use.

---

*Don't be afraid of yourself, live your individuality to
the full—but for the good of others.*

Dag Hammarskjöld,
Markings

---

*Taught from 7:30–9:00 a.m. Then at 10:30 left with
Cairns for Lusaka in their 1975 Peugeot. Ran well until
the last 80 miles when we stopped for them to repair it
about 6 times, and the last 30 miles really ran poorly,
and the last 5 miles really bad. Got here at 9:00 p.m.
Late dinner after hot bath! To bed at 11:00 p.m. It was
really a good day. Enjoyed it and felt at peace.*

May 23, 1979

Arlene and the Cairns family started out midmorning, planning to be in the capital city by suppertime. Engine trouble caused
the trip to Lusaka to be twice as long as usual, but Arlene was an
experienced rural Africa traveler, and tribulation had produced
patience. She was able to respond to the long day with joy and
gratitude, celebrating the privilege of being chauffeured through
the Zambian countryside. The browns and pinks of the scrubland
crowded the edge of the Great East Road as it tracked its way

through villages, moonscapes, and hardscrabble farms, sometimes a stone's throw from the Mozambique border. They skirted Lower Zambezi National park with its ridged hillsides and full-sized trees. With the car windows open, the ride was hot and noisy. But there was nowhere Arlene would rather be, except perhaps Ethiopia. Her heart remained in that country up north with her friends. Daily she remembered them, wondering who was in prison or facing other persecutions. Somehow, she thought, I will see them again.

The travelers arrived after dark at their intended destination, hours later than expected. There Arlene parted ways with the Cairns, who would be enjoying five days *gratis* at the Ridgeway Hotel. Their purpose in coming to the capital was for Dr. Cairns to receive a Distinction Award presented by President Kaunda himself for eighteen years of medical service in Zambia. The Cairnses dropped Arlene at the Anglican Mission, where she rested up for another journey. The next day she would be heading north to Kitwe in the Copperbelt for a conference of nursing school tutors from around the nation.

In the morning, one of the leaders at the mission compound provided Arlene with a ride to the bus station. She climbed onto a jammed-full bus at 9:25 a.m., the only Caucasian on board. Her fellow bus riders were friendly, however, and the trip was safe and uneventful. The journey took about seven hours, in part because of the five stops at police roadblocks.

What seemed like a hundred passengers spilled out of the bus at each checkpoint, lining up as an officer came down the row and examined registration cards. Once the registrations were approved, nature took its course, and what was once a roadblock became a rest stop as women huddled against the west side of the bus while men stood against the east side to relieve themselves.

Other than the heat and odor of that many people packed into a small space, it was a pleasant enough journey. The road north traversed mostly through carefully manicured and irrigated farms on long stretches of straight roadway. This route was known as the "Line of Rail" from when early in the century trains had carried copper out of the mines in the north, down through the capital, onward through Livingstone on the southern border, and all the way to the port in South Africa.

Because of the mining in that region, Kitwe is one of Zambia's most populous and cosmopolitan cities. Disembarking at the Kitwe station, Arlene caught a taxi to the north side of town, arriving at the peaceful campus of the Mindolo Ecumenical Foundation (MEF). After registering at this school and conference center, Arlene dropped her luggage in her dormitory room and made her way to the spacious dining hall.

The nurses attending the conference ate alongside the young people, who were taking leadership courses at MEF. Arlene recognized one of the young female students as Sudanese and went over to say hello. Five young men were nearby. "Where are you gentlemen from?"

"Ethiopia."

"I'm also from Ethiopia. I taught there for ten years."

One short and slight young man with a broad smile spoke up. "Where?"

"The western mountains. Mettu. Then the final year I was in Addis."

"Do you know Endalcachow?"

"Of course!"

"Tesfaye?"

"Yes."

"He's my cousin. My name is Matthew. Do you know Iteffa?"

Arlene nodded. "Do you know if he's still in prison?"

Matthew's face fell. "As far as I know. And Tadesse, too."

And on it went. He knew so many of Arlene's friends. The updates were both welcome and sobering.

After dinner as she left the hall, Matthew came over to her without the others. "Sister Arlene?"

"Matthew."

"Before you go, shall we pray for our friends facing persecution?"

"I would love that."

They sat beside the building—a middle-aged missionary and a young man in his late teens—there in Kitwe, Zambia, away from their families but brother and sister in the faith. They talked and prayed for two hours, back and forth, in an easy conversation with each other and their God. Arlene found Matthew to be remarkably kind with a self-confidence beyond his years.

Although her long weekend had been packed with meetings, on Sunday morning, her leaving day, she arranged to meet Matthew early at the school's chapel. He was waiting for her when she arrived.

"How much longer are you here, Matthew?"

"My schooling finishes in November."

"When did you arrive?"

"Last December. My pastor knew about this place and got me a scholarship. It was either come here or escape through the desert. They come for the young people first. If you don't join the Communist Party, they put you in prison to change your mind. I was in two months. Next time who knows. I have many friends who have disappeared. One can never be sure if they are runaways or in prison or dead. People are killed every night, Miss Arlene."

"I know. I saw it when I was in Addis. The gunfire could be heard after sundown. The neighborhood patrols. I seldom went out at night."

"Yes. Those are the youth of our nation turned into murderers. What will become of us if my generation is lost?"

"We must pray for them."

"Let us pray without ceasing. Shall we pray now?"

They did. Then Arlene returned to the subject of Matthew's future. "Where will you go after November? Back to Ethiopia?"

"I don't think so. If the government hasn't changed yet, to return would be suicide. I want to go, but it's not wise for now. God will tell me when."

"That is the same thing I thought about going back. So, like you, here I am in Zambia. But I have work here. What will you do after school?"

"I should continue to study. But my time here is short. This is not a college. I'd like to go to college. Everybody hopes to study overseas, Europe or America. I have little hope of that. I am a young Ethiopian in Zambia without hope. Except that the Lord is my shepherd."

"I'll continue in prayer for you, Matthew."

"Thank you, Sister Arlene."

That afternoon, on the long bus ride back to Lusaka, Arlene thought about the theme of the conference she had just attended. Fifty tutors from around Zambia had been invited. The group was told that the conference had been called because the public was not satisfied with nursing care in Zambia. Since Arlene was also dissatisfied, she felt a deep sense of vindication. She was grateful for comrades in the cause—but at the same time, she was aware that the road was long and uphill.

When her mind wandered from what they had discussed at the conference, she thought about Matthew. She was not inclined to respond to each African who sought her help to study in the United States. Matthew's story was not uncommon—a story of oppression, need, and a desire to help his people. Arlene's heart and the hearts of her Sioux Center church went out to such individuals, especially those whose stories moved beyond self-determination and included servant-leadership. Indeed, her church had already helped aspiring students who gave heartfelt promises to return home after graduation. Some of those promises had been broken, however, and the Sioux Center philanthropists had become skittish on this particular matter.

Matthew's story seemed distinctive to Arlene, and she worked to sort out why. He knew her Ethiopian friends and shared their faith and their risks. Although Arlene was similarly exiled, he was facing a greater urgency. He had, in effect, run for his life and now he was a boy without a country. Then she realized that he had actually not asked her for help. He had asked the Lord for help, and he was moving step by step in prayerful faith, expecting the Lord to guide. Arlene sensed the Lord was saying to her, "You may trust me with him. But I want you to help."

When the Peugeot had engine trouble again on the way home, Dr. Cairns guessed it was something in the gas or the gas filter. It seemed to help to simply stop and let the car rest periodically. After ten and a half hours, they limped into Katete and Arlene went to work on her Matthew problem. She wrote to a missionary friend, who then suggested a college in Nairobi. Arlene wrote several letters pursuing that option, but nothing came of it. She had $724.18 set aside as discretionary. She held it now as seed money for Matthew.

The end of the term arrived, and Matthew sent a telegram to say he was coming to visit her. He never arrived. Arlene didn't know what prevented his visit. She was caught in the usual communication disruption of a young African country in the midst of military struggles. Supplies were also unreliable, so Set 52 of her nursing students arrived at graduation day with no flour or oil to bake them a cake.

She wrote to Matthew again in mid-December with no reply. She wondered if he had returned to Ethiopia or finally decided to escape through the desert.

Meanwhile, headaches continued to plague Arlene. She visited with more than one doctor about them, and several remedies were suggested. Dr. Cairns believed it was a sinus issue, so he suggested a new codeine derivative. That provided some relief.

Then word came from home that Rev. De Jong had died. He was the beloved man of God whose sermon had brought Arlene to the point of responding, "Here am I. Send me." In her sadness and pain, she needed a respite. So, she agreed to go with the Cairns and Father Hewitt on a holiday excursion to Malawi, where they

refreshed their hearts with glorious views on the heights of the
Zambia Plateau and the banks of the 350-mile-long Lake Malawi,
one of Africa's three *Maziwa Makuu* or Great Lakes.

Upon returning to St. Francis, Arlene resumed reaching out
to Matthew. She finally learned that the dean of MEF, aware that
returning to Ethiopia was too dangerous for Matthew, had procured an extension to Matthew's scholarship. He had stayed on
for another course at MEF, and so his deadline for a decision was
extended by a few months. Arlene urged her Ethiopian friend to
visit her in Katete. She was legitimately concerned for his future and
hoped to pursue the idea of him studying in the United States. But
conversation by mail or cable was simply too unpredictable. Also,
she didn't want to raise any false hopes for him, so she invited him
under the guise of having him speak at special meetings for Nurses
Christian Fellowship.

On Monday, April 28, 1980, Arlene drove to the bus station to
pick up Charles and Partison, the two other scheduled speakers for
the NCF meetings. Matthew was due to arrive on Tuesday, so for a
second day Arlene returned to the bus station in town. But again,
no Matthew. NCF proceeded that evening with Charles preaching.

On Wednesday, when Arlene dismissed her afternoon class,
there was Matthew standing outside her door. He had taken the
train down from Kitwe two days earlier, but he had missed the bus
to Katete and had to stay in Lusaka, catching the Wednesday bus
for the long ride out to Katete. Gregarious as he was, someone at
the bus station had given him a lift over to the school. His usual
smile was still beaming, even though he had been in transit for
three days.

Arlene housed him with Charles and Partison in the *rondavel*
(traditional circular thatched hut) used as a guesthouse. On Thursday, Partison spoke at NCF, and Matthew shared his testimony on

Friday. On the final night of meetings, Auxensia, one of the male students, responded to Matthew's invitation and accepted Christ as his savior, much to Arlene's great joy.

The two soldiers returned to their camp the next morning. That Saturday Arlene had an exam to administer, after which she retired with a "wet-cloth headache." By Sunday morning, she felt a little better and accompanied Matthew to the early Communion service. This was Matthew's final full day in Katete, so Arlene committed to initiating a serious conversation about his future. They sat beside his *rondavel* and prayed and talked.

"You're not thinking of going to Ethiopia, are you?" she asked.

"No. My family told me to stay away. They love me too much to have me try to come home. Someday yes, of course. Not now."

"How much longer can you stay at Kitwe?"

"They love me there. But it's not a refugee camp. So—"

"So?"

"I need to go to college."

"Do you have a plan?"

Matthew grinned. "I have a confession to make. Do you know the big library at my school?"

"Of course. It's named after Dag Hammarskjöld."

"Yes. The United Nations leader."

"I went into that library the weekend I first met you," she said.

"His plane crashed close to my school in Kitwe."

She nodded. "I saw the sign to the memorial from my bus."

"He was a very important man for the world. I spend all my extra time in that library. They have information about colleges. I go there reaching for a lifeline. Every day. No wasted time. I have looked all over Africa. And Europe. And they have one book, a thick book, full of colleges in America. I have written to many. I wrote to one in Nebraska." Matthew struggled to pronounce the name of the town, "Fraymount?"

Arlene helped him with the pronunciation, "*Free*mont."

"You've heard of it?"

"Dr. Mary Smith lives a few miles from there. She was a doctor at Mettu."

"At Mettu?! God is good."

"What's the name of the college in Fremont?"

"It's a Christian college—Midland Lutheran. I sent for an application, and they sent, and I sent, and I have a surprise."

Arlene's heart swelled at this, but she braced herself and cautiously asked, "What surprise, Matthew?"

"I am accepted to attend Christian college in Fremont, Nebraska. I owe them a deposit of $1,000. And then $4,000 more for the first year of college."

"Wow. And that's also a long ways to swim."

Matthew laughed. "Oh yes. A plane ticket, too. But first things first. I'm accepted!"

"I'm sorry, Matthew. I should have said that's wonderful. You're accepted to college! I'm so happy for you." And she was, but she felt other emotions too.

"So, will you pray with me for the next step, Arlene?"

"I will." They prayed, in gratitude and hope. And as they prayed, Arlene was deciding. When they finished with "Amen," she said, "I know someone I'm going to write to. I don't know what will happen, but I'll write."

"You're going to ask them to help me?"

"Yes, I am. We'll see. Do you know what you plan to study?"

"Well . . . after all this trouble, my country will need leaders. The college has a major in Business Administration that seems good."

Arlene nodded and then added a detail she knew would commit her. "Did you know that Fremont is only about two hours by car from my Iowa home?"

"That's wonderful!" said Matthew. "I can meet your people."

Later that day, a truck was heading into Lusaka from the hospital. Arlene wrote a brief letter to Ma and Grada and sent it along for mailing in the capital. She asked Grada to tip off Gerrett and

Margaret Schutt to look for a letter from her. The Schutts were farmers and members of Arlene's home church. Arlene had identified them as having the wherewithal to give Matthew substantial help. She knew that their respect for her would add significance to the request. She planned to pay the deposit of one-thousand dollars herself, but she told no one other than Grada.

On Monday, Arlene drove Matthew to the bus station. She wondered what road she had started down. That night she had a hard time getting to sleep.

The goal—to help an Ethiopian boy survive and grow up to be a leader among his people—was a bit audacious and would require money for tuition, housing, food, expenses, and travel. Then there was the unpredictable obstacle of immigration. There would be forms to obtain, forms to complete, and a visa that could be procured only by paying a nonrefundable fee, followed by a personal interview with the ambassador at the U.S. Embassy in Lusaka. It was no wonder that besides having a two-week stretch of headaches every day, Arlene often woke up in the middle of the night with Matthew on her mind.

She was like the boy Samuel who had begun his calling by responding to an awakening in the middle of the night with the words, "Speak, for your servant is listening." When Arlene woke in the night, she listened by reading Scripture and asking the Lord for whom and what she should pray. Later when she rose for the day, she started her journal entries such as,

God awakens me early, sometimes at 3 or 4, to read and pray. He gives me strength.

This was good, because she would require much strengthening that summer of 1980.

Arlene instructed her sister to withdraw $1,000 from her personal account and send it to Midland for Matthew's deposit. It was her understanding that this action would set an important process in motion. The college would send Matthew an I-20 Form that affirmed him as an enrolled student. He must then display that form during his visa application as well as to Border Control. Arlene repeated her instructions to Grada twice during the following month, since she could never be certain which letters or telegrams actually got through. But she didn't need to repeat this request, because Grada had acted promptly and the I-20 arrived at Kitwe in plenty of time.

By the Thursday following Matthew's Monday departure, Arlene had carefully typed up her request to the Schutts. She worked to finish the letter by Thursday, because the Cairns were heading to Lusaka. Arlene sent her letter along to the capital city's Chachacha Road Post Office with a whispered prayer: "God, either make his going or not going crystal clear." In actuality, she believed his going was clear and she was acting on that belief. Nevertheless, she valued a submissive faith and did not perceive such openness as doubt.

Matthew and Arlene had held their serious Sunday morning conversation on May 4. One month to the day—on June 4, 1980—a cable was delivered to the hospital for Arlene from Sioux Center:

ARRANGEMENT IS MADE FOR MATTHEW PLEASE
PROCEED SINCERELY GERRETT SCHUTT

Arlene raced back to the telegraph office to send a cable to Matthew, but by the time she got there, the office was closed. The next day, at her earliest break from teaching, Arlene returned to the telegraph office.

AMERICAN CABLE ARRIVED YESTERDAY
ARRANGEMENTS AGREED PROCEED WITH
ALL YOUR PLANS AND PRAISE GOD

She wished she could have been there to see his face.

Arlene knew the Schutts, and she knew the wealth of her home church. If she and the Schutts ran out of financial resources for Matthew, there were others to ask. Indeed, others were asked. In keeping with their Dutch community, those others were also named Schutt or Schut. Although Pete and Gladys Schut were not related to Gerrett and Margaret Schutt, they were Arlene's favorite cousins. They lived just two doors north of Ma and Grada on Second Avenue. Pete and Gladys would do anything for Arlene. They were the ones who had leapt at the chance to pick up Arlene in Omaha when she flew home from Hyden for Pa's funeral. Now, twenty years later, they had somehow caught wind of the project and were eager to join. Pete and Gerrett drove down to Fremont to check out the school and speak to the admissions officers. They confirmed that tuition, room, and board totaled $5,000 a year and that someone had already paid the deposit. Assuming additional expenses for books and supplies, the men decided they would together place $4,400 more into Matthew's account for his first year.

Matthew was unaware of the Gerrett and Pete's decision and of the joyful givers who occupied the pews of Arlene's church. All he knew at this point was that his deposit had been paid so he could start school. Matthew had a step-by-step faith. "PROCEED WITH ALL YOUR PLANS" meant to Matthew that he should, well, proceed! His next step was to secure a plane ticket, so he began to pray for transportation.

One evening, Mr. Ajea, the dean of MEF who had extended Matthew's stay, had a pastor friend visiting from Canada. One night, they invited Matthew to join them for dinner.

The pastor had been to Ethiopia and was curious to hear about Matthew's experiences. Finally, the pastor grew concerned. "May

I ask you a serious question? You're not thinking of going back there, are you?"

"Well, it's dangerous, but it is my home. And there comes a time when all of us must put our trust in the Lord."

"No, Matthew. Don't go to Ethiopia." He spoke quite sternly. "The young people are killing each other. I've seen the bodies in the streets."

Matthew looked at the dean for permission to share more.

Mr. Ajea said, "Go ahead, Matthew. Tell him."

"All right. There is a woman, a friend who teaches in Katete, who has found the money for my college in America. That's a start. But I don't yet have a plane ticket. So," he pointed to the dean with a smile, "your friend, Mr. Ajea, and I have agreed here on earth to ask our Father in heaven for a plane ride."

The pastor looked at them and nodded. "Tomorrow I'm returning to my church in Canada. I'll see if anyone there would like to agree with your prayer."

A week later, Mr. Ajea called Matthew into his office. "Do you remember my pastor friend?"

"The man who ordered me not to go home?"

"Yes, him. His church has purchased your plane ticket. You can go to Nebraska."

Matthew stared, shook his head, and finally broke into one of his broadest smiles. "God has answered our prayers, Mr. Ajea."

"I should say so. I'm going to miss you, Matthew. I hope you'll return some day."

The money question was solved far beyond Matthew's understanding. Leatta stunned Arlene by adding a $500 check to give to him before he left the country with strict instructions that he was to cash it at a bank in Fremont and use it to buy some winter clothes.

But there were other challenges looming. Matthew wrote to Arlene that he now believed he would need something called an "Affidavit of Support" when he went to apply for his visa. He would not be permitted to get a visa without having a financially solvent person living in America, who promised to keep him from becoming a government dependent once he entered the country. Arlene sent a cable to Gerrett, hoping he would agree to complete the form and send it back to the U.S. Embassy in Lusaka.

Since college started at the end of August, the final step in getting Matthew there on time was to procure a visa—that step was Matthew's to take. Although Arlene guessed she might not be allowed to attend his interview at the embassy, she thought it would be best if she at least made herself available. She wrote to Matthew that she had General Nursing Council meetings in Lusaka in early July. If he could travel down to Lusaka, she would be ready to go with him to the embassy on July 10.

In early July, the GNC moved its meetings to a week later. Arlene hurried to cable Matthew a new date to meet at the embassy. But by the time her cable arrived in Kitwe, Matthew was already on the train headed south.

On July 10, Matthew waited for Arlene until he could wait no longer, then he went into the embassy alone. He carried the admission letter and Form I-20 he had received from his American college. He had his passport, and in his wallet was the visa application fee. Matthew could only hope that the ambassador had received the Affidavit of Support. After signing in at the reception desk, he waited for his name to be called.

Workers bustled back and forth, carrying files and trays of tea. Matthew had never been inside such a beautiful building with its shiny floors, high ceilings, and echoing sounds. Suddenly, he heard his name called, and he sprang to his feet.

"Follow me," said a young man about Matthew's age. They went through a door, down a hall, and into another waiting area filled with people writing on pieces of paper attached to clipboards. The young man picked up a clipboard from a counter and handed it to Matthew. "Fill this out and let someone know when you're finished," he said and left.

Matthew sat down and carefully completed the form. He double-checked it and then stood, waiting to let someone know. After several sets of young men in uniforms hurried through the room, Matthew stopped one of them and held out his form. The uniformed man took it without looking at it and disappeared down a hallway. Matthew wondered if he should follow, but he decided to sit down and wait.

Other people were called and disappeared down a hallway. Some of them returned with smiles, and some returned with stone faces. Matthew was more than ready when the uniformed man returned and beckoned to follow him down the hall. At an open doorway, the uniformed man paused, gestured, and disappeared.

Matthew looked into the small room. There was a window on the opposite wall. The window was open, and the drapes moved a little in the afternoon breeze. On the wall with the window were shelves piled high with folders. The room also held a desk and a few chairs. Behind the desk sat a man. This must be the American ambassador, Matthew thought. He was light-skinned and seemed to be have an Asian background. He was looking at some papers in front of him, which Matthew recognized as his papers. Matthew moved toward a chair opposite the man behind the desk.

"Don't sit down," he said.

"I'm sorry," Matthew said.

"You've come to the wrong place."

"Excuse me?"

"You're an Ethiopian?"

"Yes. I'm here in Zambia going to school."

"Right. So you have to go to the U.S. Embassy in Addis Ababa to obtain your visa."

"What?"

"You have to go the U.S. Embassy in—"

"No, I cannot go there. It is too dangerous for me."

"Well, if you can't go there, you can't get a visa. That's the rule."

Matthew swallowed hard. "Is there anything else I can do?"

"I don't make the rules."

Matthew tried one more thing. "Do you have . . . do you . . . have you received an Affidavit of Support for me from someone in America?"

"No, we have no Affidavit of Support for you. I'm sorry, now you'll have to excuse me."

"May I have my application back?"

"No, we keep that on file."

Matthew didn't even bother to make a stone face as he passed through the hallways and reception areas. He was awash in tears. When he made it past the guards, the gate, and onto the street, he became *Mosi-oa-Tunya* ("The Smoke That Thunders"), and all who heard him knew his hope was destroyed and his heart was broken.

On Monday morning, July 14, as Matthew boarded his train to return to Kitwe, Arlene drove out of Katete toward Lusaka. It was a beautiful day. She stopped at the Nyimba petrol station, paying about $4.25 per gallon in U.S. dollars. She realized the price was ridiculously high, but the alternative was the bus, which would mean depending on taxis in the city. Given the news that the Lusaka Strangler had been terrorizing the capital since January, she thought it best to have her own safer means of transportation.

She reached Lusaka at 12:15. After lunch, she went off on a search. Although she had planned to meet Matthew at the American Embassy two days from now, she was hoping to lay a little groundwork by contacting Bereket Eyoas, a United Nations diplomat from Ethiopia who was living in exile in Zambia after escaping the Communists in his home country. If anyone would understand Matthew's plight, Bereket would. Perhaps he could help. She drove to several locations Monday afternoon but could not find Mr. Eyoas.

She checked in at the YWCA where she would be staying during her meetings with the General Nursing Council. Wednesday would be a light day with the GNC, so that was the day she had set aside to connect with Matthew at the U.S. Embassy. Would they find each other? She could not be sure.

"Gichile!"

Someone was calling his last name as he walked in from the train station onto the Mindolo campus that Monday evening. Matthew didn't want to see his friends and teachers yet. He didn't want to meet Mr. Ajea. How could he tell them without crying that he had once again become the Ethiopian boy living in Zambia without hope? How could he admit to the pastor from Canada that his plane ticket would be used to fly to Addis Ababa?

"Matthew!"

He finally looked up and saw a tall classmate from the Sudan. He was holding half a sheet of paper in his hand.

"The white lady sent you a telegram," the tall classmate said. "She wants you to meet her in Lusaka."

"What? I just came from Lusaka."

"Look at the paper. She wants you to meet her on Wednesday to go the embassy."

"I'm just coming from there."

"Go back!"

Matthew started to cry. "It won't do any good! They've already rejected my application. It's over."

"No! She is an American. She knows something you don't know. She invited you to meet her. Go!"

"I'm so tired."

"Get some sleep, then hop on tomorrow's train to be sure to get there in time."

There was nothing in Matthew that wanted to return to Lusaka. He was not even sure how to find Arlene in that great city. The arrangements had already failed once. But, he thought, he was an Ethiopian boy living in Zambia without any hope. Staying in Kitwe or taking the train to Lusaka were similar things to him. So, at his friend's command, he said his prayers, slept, and returned to the train station.

Despite a few late-night drunken people noising around at the YWCA, Arlene was able to get enough rest to rouse herself at 5:30 for morning prayer, committing the day to the Lord. When she arrived at the GNC offices around 9:00, she discovered that the Examination Committee meetings had been moved to the next day, Wednesday. But that was the day she had told Matthew to meet her at the U.S. Embassy. Disappointed, she decided to at least investigate whether the Affidavit of Support had arrived and then to say whatever she could on his behalf. She resigned herself to the understanding that Matthew would have to do the remainder on his own when he applied on Wednesday without her. She headed toward the embassy.

Since the YWCA was located between the GNC and the embassy, she stopped there for lunch and then continued the five miles to the embassy compound. She introduced herself as an American citizen wanting to speak with someone about a Matthew Gichile. The receptionist asked her to wait, and before long, a uniformed young man led her into an office.

The man there was a Zambian national sitting at his desk looking at a file. He barely looked up. "You're here on behalf of someone else?"

"Yes. A Matthew Gichile," Arlene answered as she sat down.

"You cannot apply on his behalf."

"I understand that. I was here to ask if you had received—"

The embassy official cut her off. "Did you know his visa application has already been turned down?"

"No . . . I did not know that. How is that possible? He's supposed to meet me here tomorrow to make the application."

"He was here last week."

"He was?"

"I have his file."

"I don't understand."

The official held out a piece of paper. There was Matthew's name and personal information in the handwriting Arlene recognized from his letters. The man asked, "Is that your man?"

Arlene nodded.

"There's the date. There's the officer's decision. Have his circumstances changed?"

Arlene said that she would try to speak with Matthew.

"Are we finished, ma'am?"

Arlene nodded and stood.

As Arlene left the embassy, the train from Kitwe pulled into Lusaka Railway Station. When Matthew climbed down from the train onto the platform, he realized he was a day early to meet Arlene, but he decided to start looking for her right away. He asked for directions to the General Nursing Council offices and learned that it was a twenty-minute walk straight up Cairo Road from the train station. He walked some and ran some, arriving about 4:00 p.m.

The guard stopped him. "Sorry, the building's closing for the day."

"I believe a friend of mine is having meetings here."

"Well, the meetings are all done today."

"All right," Matthew said, turning away. Then he turned back. "Did you see a white lady here for the meetings?"

"Sure. Three or four of them."

"Which way did they go?"

The guard pointed and Matthew ran. But he saw no white women. Ahead of him was an open-air market where he saw the largest crowd of black faces he had seen yet in that great city. He kept going and suddenly he saw a flash of white—it was a white woman getting out of a car. He fixed his eyes on her and moved forward. Her face turned toward him and then broke into a smile. It was Arlene. He began to cry.

As he came close, she said, "I know, Matthew, I heard they turned you down."

"But you were not there, Miss Arlene. Maybe when you go with me tomorrow, things will be different."

"I can't. I can't go with you tomorrow, Matthew."

"Why not?"

"They've changed my meeting schedule. If you had looked for me tomorrow, you would not have seen me. I'm so sorry. I just found out this morning. But I believe the Lord has brought us together today. The embassy is still open. Can you go right now?"

"Do zebras have stripes?" said Matthew. As he stepped around her car, he let himself feel a pinch of hope.

On the way across the city during afternoon rush hour, they exchanged stories of their previous visits to the embassy. And they prayed.

"What's the purpose of your visit?" asked the guard at the embassy gate.

"This young man is here to get his visa."

"Well, I think all the visa appointments are done for today. You should try again tomorrow."

"I can't return with him tomorrow. Could you please let us try today?

"I can let you through the gate, but I can't promise anyone inside will see you."

Arlene thanked the guard and drove on through. "Keep walking and praying, Matthew," she said as they got out of the car.

Inside the building, the offices were quieting down. Arlene told a receptionist that they wished to speak with an ambassador about Matthew Gichile's visa application and that she had new information for his case. Although they had to wait again, it didn't take as long as before. When the familiar uniformed worker gestured Matthew and Arlene into the final office, a different person sat behind the desk. He invited them to sit.

"I spoke with someone earlier today," Arlene said.

"And I spoke with someone last week," Matthew added.

The official smiled and said, "I hopped across the Pond last week—just started this morning. You've caught me on my very first day."

Arlene said, "Welcome to Zambia."

The man said, "Well, technically this embassy is considered American soil."

"Yes, of course. Welcome to America inside Zambia."

"I take it you're from America."

"I grew up in Iowa, yes. But I've been a nurse and teacher on the African continent for twenty-five years."

"You like it here?"

"Yes, I do."

"Then I hope I feel the same, especially if I stay as long as you. How may I help you today?"

"We're here to explain some new circumstances about Matthew's visa application."

"May I have the application?" the man asked.

"They kept it," said Matthew.

The man stood up and left the room. Arlene and Matthew looked at each other, and then they both bowed their heads, praying with their eyes open.

The man returned, flipping through the pages. "It says you've come to the wrong embassy. Are you Ethiopian?"

"Yes, sir."

"I'm guessing Ethiopia's a bit dangerous right now."

"Yes, sir."

"So you'd like to enter America from here."

"Yes, sir."

"Which is technically against the rules. Do you have your Affidavit of Support?"

Arlene quickly spoke up. "If it's not in the file, I believe it's on the way. But I'm willing to guarantee his support."

"On what basis?"

"I've known him for over a year. I lived near his hometown in Ethiopia for ten years. We know many of the same people. He and I have both been forced to leave the land we love. We have the same faith and have prayed together many times for Ethiopia and its people."

The man turned to Matthew. "And you want to study in the United States?"

"Yes, sir."

"Do you hope to stay there?"

"I hope to return to my country."

"After it's safe?"

"Yes, sir."

"Arlene, do you trust this boy?"

The words she spoke next confirmed Matthew's calling: "Sometimes people who want to emigrate say what they think we want to hear. But he and I have spoken freely, and I believe him. He will get his education and come back to Africa and serve his people."

The man looked at the Ethiopian boy for a long time. Then he said, "I believe her, Matthew. If you come back here tomorrow, I'll grant your visa. Ask specifically for me by name. And get your Affidavit of Support. I can't guarantee you'll get through customs without it."

Since Arlene did not have meetings the following Sunday, she agreed to worship with Matthew and the family hosting him while he was in Lusaka. They met at an English-speaking Assemblies of God church. Two things happened at the church that morning that made Arlene wonder if God had his own reasons for everything that occurred that week.

First, during those few days in Lusaka, Matthew had located Bereket Eyoas, the expatriate Ethiopian diplomat. He invited Bereket to church that morning, and he arrived at the church with his wife Amaklech. That morning, they responded to an invitation to receive the gospel and became Christ-followers. Second, during the service, Arlene happened to sit next to a woman who introduced herself as Vi Nissley.

When Arlene spoke her own name, Vi surprised her by saying, "Arlene Schuiteman? Oh! We were just talking about you. I work for CMAZ (Churches Medical Association of Zambia) and Sylvia Chesterman said, 'I think it's time we get in touch with Arlene about transferring to Macha—their need is greater than Katete now.'"

Arlene's heart leapt. She had always felt her real call to Zambia was at Macha. There was, of course, no official decision that morning, but a seed was planted that immediately began to grow.

Arlene wrote to Gerrett a second time, and by the end of July, she had the Affidavit of Support (Gerrett had never received her telegram). Arlene calculated a way to bypass the unreliable postal system and have the affidavit delivered personally to Matthew through her missionary network. She also arranged for relatives of hers who lived in Omaha to meet Matthew's plane and care for him until the day they would accompany him to his dorm at Midland Lutheran College.

Matthew's first semester of college was both wonderful and difficult. He had assumed that Arlene was a typical American and that all his college classmates would be followers of Jesus. In his first speech assignment, he eagerly shared his testimony and was shocked by the cold response until another classmate whispered, "Praise the Lord. Me too."

He quickly realized his own naivety about America as well as college, but he continued to wear his faith on his sleeve and his candor was winsome. Guys in his dorm stopped by his room to ask, "Matthew, will you teach me how to pray?" The Bible study he led in his room was soon crowded, and churches around Fremont invited him to speak to their youth groups. His schedule filled, and that overcommitment—along with the challenge of studying in a second language—spiraled his grades downward. He persevered, however, and graduated with a BA from Midland Lutheran College (now University) and an MBA from Oklahoma City University. At the time of this writing, he is about to complete his PhD. He and his wife, Melatwork Hailu (who has an MBA from Harvard University and a law degree from Addis Ababa University), have two children.

Matthew kept his promise to Africa. He went to work for the United Nations, serving the East African countries of Kenya, Uganda, and Tanzania. By the early 1990s, Communism was collapsing in Ethiopia. When Mengistu fled to Zimbabwe, Matthew headed home. There he discovered that only 10 percent of Ethiopia's high school graduates continued on to higher education. In keeping with his concern for his nation's young people, he became the founding president of New Generation University College. Less than two decades after its opening in 2002, NGUC has four campuses on the African continent serving some 9,000 students a year at undergraduate and graduate levels.

As for Arlene and Matthew, they have remained lifelong friends.

12

Iteffa

Awumwi ulanzembelo yakwe.
Each and every one has a different war dance.

The long awaited but unexpected day of once again returning to Ethiopia. Bob and Morrie took me to the airport. Arrived on Kenya Airways at 3 p.m. No problem. New airport in use. Pictures greet you of Lenin, Engels, and Marx. Dottie, Iteffa, and Daniel meet me. They made me a feast of injera ba wat. God, I do thank you. Memories, memories. Tadesse tells of torture in prison.

September 17, 1980

On September 12, 1980, Arlene rose at 4:00 a.m. in Katete, knowing she would soon be able to catch up on a lot of lost sleep. Almost a year ago, just before Glenn Bruggers (Arlene's Reformed church missions supervisor) visited, Faith Cairns commented, "Bruggers will take the whip to us for not giving you any vacation in fifteen months."

Finally, a three-month furlough was about to commence. This furlough, Glenn had insisted, was not to be crammed with deputation work—it was to be a time for Arlene to recuperate after such a long and heavy season of daily exertion. Part of this recuperation was needed because Dr. Cairns had recommended sinus surgery for Arlene in an attempt to alleviate her long-standing headache problem.

Leatta stayed at the nursing school to help orient Arlene's replacement, and Leatta's own furlough would come soon enough. Although Arlene would be heading home to Sioux Center for most of her furlough, she had a week set aside to stop first in Addis Ababa. Since it wasn't safe for her to travel to Mettu, her former home in the western Ethiopian mountains, many of her friends would meet her in the capital. Her eagerness to once again embrace her friends who had faced great persecution was almost overwhelming.

Ever since she left Ethiopia in 1977, she had been tracking—mostly via coded letters and the missionary "grapevine"—the movement of her Ethiopian friends in and out of prison. She now read the New Testament with greater understanding. The imprisonments of Paul, Peter, and others came to vivid reality as her own friends shared in the sufferings of those first followers of Christ. Phrases such as "ambassador in chains" and "the mystery of Christ, for which I am in prison" gained new potency, and the roll call of the faithful in Hebrews 11 now seemed to include her own friends.

Especially important to Arlene was the well-being of her evangelist friend Iteffa. When Arlene had experienced confusion after receiving the gift of speaking in tongues, Iteffa managed to draw her attention away from the gift and back to the Giver. He was also the one who sent the coded message when she was considering returning to Ethiopia—hinting that he was about to enter prison and unsure if he would ever make it back out.

Imprisoned in early 1978, Iteffa was released after five and a half months. That reprieve lasted less than two months, however, and before the year ended, he was back behind bars.

By early May 1979, Arlene heard that persecution was "really, really bad" in Ethiopia. Those who refused to denounce God or religion sometimes were simply shot. Others were imprisoned, which is what happened to Iteffa that same month. By June 1980, word came that he had been released. He had been in for a total of one year and seven months.

On September 18, 1980, fellow missionary Dottie picked up Arlene at the mission guesthouse and drove across Addis Ababa to the Mexico Square area, one of the well-known traffic circles. Just beyond the circle, they parked and walked to Iteffa's home where he lived with his wife, Alamaz. Four additional friends were there, and they all listened as Iteffa revealed what prison life was like for a pastor who was in conflict with a Communist government.

In prison, Iteffa had shared a small, windowless cell with many other prisoners but no furniture. They had to cope with two levels of authority. The first was the prison guards and their weapons, and the second was the chaos of prisoner relationships—which ranged from kindness to atrocity.

Sometimes Iteffa was removed by the guards from the group cell. Of course, this could mean that he was being released—there was always that hope. But typically, what at first was a welcome break from the group cell drama turned to horror as he arrived at an interrogation room. Handcuffed to a chain suspended from the ceiling, Iteffa's full weight pulled on his wrists. He was left like that for what he guessed was about three hours. Sometimes they placed a pole under his knees, suspending him upside down. This enabled them to beat the bottoms of his feet. During his torture, he tried to remain quiet to avoid having a gag shoved in his mouth—which was sometimes a rag filled with human feces.

After his final release, Iteffa walked with a limp for weeks and his hands were numb for three months. In addition to all this, he felt that transitioning to outside society was difficult enough to be a new kind of torture.

Iteffa told the group gathered in his living room that Thursday how the Lord had been in jail with him. Arlene copied down his words: "The Lord blessed me there, and the blessings surpassed all the suffering."

While Arlene was in Addis, many friends came to find her, and a group from Mettu called her on the phone. She bought an Ethiopian shirt to take to Matthew in Nebraska to remind him of home. On her final night, some friends read aloud from 2 Thessalonians 3:1–5 as an epilogue to her long-awaited but unexpected return to them in Ethiopia:

> Pray for us that the word of the Lord will spread quickly and be honored here just as it is with you. Pray that we may be rescued from wicked and evil people. Not everyone has faith. But the Lord is faithful. May our God strengthen you and protect you from evil. We trust the Lord concerning you that you will continue doing what we have asked. May the Lord direct your passions into continuing love of God and patient waiting for Christ.

13

Strangler

Buunsi bwakabi mbumwi.
It takes only a day for things to get spoiled.

---

*Bernice took me to Orange City to vote absentee and to
Grossman to check lymph gland. He ordered X-ray and
am to report back after I get back from Michigan and
New York. Halloween and about 40 kids came to door.*

October 31, 1980

Arlene was home on furlough during the U.S. presidential election that pitted Ronald Reagan against incumbent Jimmy Carter. Arlene's sister closest in age, Bernice, picked her up from the brick house on Second Avenue to drive twelve miles to the courthouse in Orange City to cast her ballot early. On election day, she would be on a short tour out East, visiting supporting churches, and she wouldn't be home until just before Thanksgiving.

While in Orange City on that last day of October, she had an appointment with a surgeon to see if he was as concerned as she was about a lump. She'd had a cancer scare during her time in Ethiopia when medical consultation was difficult to access. Therefore, she was eager to address this concern while she was in the States. Dr. Grossman sent her to the hospital for an X-ray and said he would report the results when she returned from her trip. She was not especially pleased to be lugging that concern all the way to the Atlantic coast and back, but what could she do?

That night, Arlene and Grada took turns carrying the big candy dish to the door as dozens of church and neighborhood friends stood back and smiled as their children rang the doorbell and yelled, "Trick or treat!" It was a ridiculous and delightful tradition, and Arlene was glad to be home for it this year.

That same day back at St. Francis, Leatta sat at her desk typing a letter to Arlene. In it, she revealed the long-awaited answer to the horrifying mystery that had haunted their lives and those of their students for nearly a year.

At the start of the nightmare, there had been no sense that a killing spree had begun. January 5, 1980, seemed to be a normal Saturday, and Arlene's journal entry for that day in Katete listed routine events:

Washed. Cleaned. Exam plus returned papers. Working in school until 1:30 p.m. so short afternoon. Big ironing. Washed hair. Wrote 2 letters. We canned mango jam at night. New students arriving.

In Lusaka that morning, though, a young woman's body was found at the edge of a grade school soccer field. The Criminal Investigation Department (CID) discovered she was from Sinazongwe, a small town on the northern shore of Lake Kariba, the world's largest man-made lake, created by the Kariba Dam on the Zambezi River between Zambia and Zimbabwe. She carried a train ticket to Kitwe, north of the capital. It was not clear how she had been killed or when. Perhaps it was a robbery gone wrong. Theft was a serious problem in Zambia, and sometimes this included violence. Perhaps it was a romance turned sour or a domestic dispute. The only clues were that at some point she had been at the train station, she was a young woman, and her body had been left where it would be easily found.

By the end of January, six women had been killed in Lusaka—
the majority of them under similar circumstances. The cause of
death was most often cited as strangulation, leading the press to
call the murderer "The Lusaka Strangler."

News arrived at Katete in fits and starts, sometimes by radio via
the Voice of America (VOA) or the British Broadcasting Corpora-
tion (BBC). Sometimes Lusaka newspapers arrived at the hospital
and were passed around. People traveling from Lusaka, of course,
could personally report what they heard in the city. Rumor and
misinformation abounded.

The fairly accurate details were that the victims had connections
to the train, the bus, or hotels. The bodies were not usually hidden,
and some of the victims' personal belongings were scattered near
them, suggesting that the motive was not robbery. Many of the
victims had been sexually assaulted. By the end of February, there
were about a dozen deaths attributed to the Strangler. Fear gripped
the city, and the government imposed a dusk-to-dawn curfew. A
month later, the rumor was that twenty-eight women had been
killed by either one man or by a gang of stranglers. One conspiracy
theory Arlene heard was that traditional medicine men needed
female hearts to formulate their concoctions.

In late March, Arlene had General Nursing Council meetings
in Lusaka. She rearranged the school schedule, gave her students
their exams early, and sent everyone off on spring break with strict
warnings to be careful. Leatta attended the meetings with her, and at
their close, the women drove south on an excursion to Macha and
then on to Victoria Falls. The final leg of their journey fell during
Holy Week. On Maundy Thursday, they were cruising northeast on
the Great East Road between Lusaka and Katete.

They couldn't have known that during that same weekend, one
of their students, Regina Mumba, was moving along the Line of
Rail southward on a late bus. Besides being a nursing student, she
was a wife and mother of three little boys. She had spent spring

break at home in Kitwe, and now, on her way back to school, she was planning to spend a couple of days with her in-laws in Lusaka. Regina never made it to the home of her in-laws. On Easter Sunday, she was found strangled to death in an alley near the city airport.

The following Wednesday, feeling puny, Arlene recognized the onset of some illness. She nevertheless went to the office, gave a tour to some visiting dignitaries from a school in Chipata, attended a staff meeting, and delivered a lecture to her late afternoon class. Regina was not in attendance. After class, the truth spread through the school. The Strangler had struck one of their own. Arlene called the police to make sure they knew. The police eventually showed up at the school to interview Regina's friends and teachers. The Katete authorities then sent the results of their inquiries to the Lusaka detectives, who were frantically trying to end this nightmare.

Through that spring and summer, Arlene continued to travel in and out of Lusaka for the General Nursing Council. She used her car, thus avoiding public transportation, and did not travel after dark. She acknowledged the presence of danger, and she was as careful as she should be, but she was not afraid.

As Arlene was packing for her furlough, the murders continued. On Sunday, September 7, she went to the 6:30 a.m. Communion service at the Anglican Chapel, praying that her student's killer would be stopped.

That same morning, up in the Copperbelt, Josephine Mukatasha went to the Chingola bus station with a suitcase and her little girl, a toddler. They had a long day of travel ahead. They rode south to Kitwe and then transferred to a Lusaka-bound bus. At Ndola, they passed the turn-off to the famous Hammarskjöld memorial. Josephine befriended a girl heading to Petauke but did not later remember her name.

The bus arrived late into Lusaka—at a quarter after ten. Josephine's connecting bus to Mumbwa was long gone. She would have to find a place for her and her daughter to spend the night. Her daughter had already fallen asleep and was tied with a *chitenge* to her mother's back.

Josephine decided they would lie down at the empty bus station and try to get some rest.

Just then, a man in a soldier's uniform approached her and said sternly, "Let me see your identification card."

She handed him her card.

He looked at it. "Mrs.?"

"Yes, sir."

"Where's your husband?"

"He didn't travel with us."

"Mrs. Mukatasha, are you planning to sleep here tonight?"

"I thought we might."

He handed back her identification.

"Why don't you follow me? There's a rest house over there, and I'll make the arrangements for you to be comfortable, you and your girl."

The man seemed very polite. And he had a uniform. She had heard of the Lusaka Strangler, though, so she said, "We'll be fine here. But thank you very much."

The man in the uniform smiled and moved away. After a while he returned. "You know, I've already helped someone to the rest house tonight. They're probably already sound asleep. Are you sure you won't let me help you? You'd be silly to sleep here. It's not safe."

She thought he was right. He was being kind, and she was being silly. She nodded.

"Wait a minute. Wait right here." He left, and she saw him jog over to a little drink shop. Soon he was back with two orange Fantas, one for her and one for the little girl. The little girl was asleep, so she pulled her out of the fabric wrapping and woke her. The little girl took the bottle, and the man picked up the suitcase and began to walk away. Josephine sighed, hitched her girl up onto her hip, and followed.

They walked and walked. The little girl fell back asleep, and Josephine handed the Fanta bottles back to the man. He tossed them to the side of the road. They walked some more, and then the man turned off onto a dark path.

Josephine stopped. "Where are we going?"

The man in the uniform pointed toward a light in the distance.

Josephine decided to wrap up her girl and transfer her to her back. As she did, the man moved around behind her. She thought he wanted to help, but suddenly his hands clenched her neck, and she knew she had made a terrible mistake. Then she lost consciousness.

Out in Katete that Sunday night, Bible study was finishing up. Twelve nurses were there, and that evening they had completed their study of the book of Genesis when Joseph makes his brothers swear, saying to them, "When God comes to help you and lead you back, you must take my bones with you."

A baby was crying. Someone's baby was crying. *Her* baby was crying. Josephine opened her eyes. Her little girl was lying next to her, wailing. She turned her head and looked around, and then sat up. They appeared to be alone. Her suitcase was gone, her wristwatch was gone, and her wedding ring was gone. But she and her daughter were alive.

Suddenly, she felt sick.

After she vomited, she wrapped up her girl, swung her to her back, and walked toward some houses, calling for help.

At the start of her furlough, Arlene was traveling through Lusaka on September 12 and 13. She didn't know that on those very days, elsewhere in the city, a woman named Josephine was helping the police craft a sting operation to capture the Strangler.

Josephine Mukatasha had given the police her statement. Yes, she was sure she could identify him if she saw him again. Yes, she was willing to help in any way she could to stop the Lusaka Strangler.

Yes, she did have an idea why she was left alive. "It was the providence of God," she said.

An audacious plan was hatched. Astoundingly, Josephine herself would be the bait. She would return to the bus station at night—without her little girl, of course. The police would be waiting for her signal when she saw the same man.

Before the day of the sting, Arlene flew out of Lusaka. On September 16, she was in Nairobi at the Ethiopian Embassy. In the late afternoon, the Ethiopian ambassador finally handed Arlene the longed-for visa by which she could return to Addis Ababa.

About that same hour that same afternoon, a Lusaka police detective was traveling with Josephine in an unmarked car to drop her off near the intercity bus station.

After walking to the station, Josephine stood by the buses and wandered back and forth, trying to appear a bit lost. The bait was not in the water long.

At 6:30 p.m., she heard a familiar voice. "Hey . . . do I know you from somewhere?"

She turned around and looked again into the face of the Lusaka Strangler. She didn't panic. Instead, she giggled. "I don't think so. I'm not from here."

"I thought you looked a little lost. Where are you from?"

"Chingola." That was the truth.

"Up north? Copper mine town?"

She nodded and smiled pleasantly, moving her *chitenge* from her shoulders to her head. Where were the police? Couldn't they see that she was giving them the sign?

"Have you found your rest house for tonight yet?"

She nearly threw up. She swallowed hard, kept smiling, and shook her head.

"Why don't you follow me?" the man in the uniform said. "There's a rest house over there, and I'll make arrangements for you to be comfortable tonight."

"Okay. That sounds good. But can you wait for me while I run over there and collect my baggage?"

"Sure, okay."

"You won't leave, will you?"

"I'll stay right here."

"Good! Great!"

And that was how Josephine Mukatasha led the police directly to the perpetrator they had been hunting for months—the Lusaka Strangler. This man had her watch on his wrist, her ring in his pocket, and many other keepsakes from his victims at his home. One item recovered had belonged to a Regina Mumba, who had been a nursing student in Katete.

On Thursday of that week, Arlene was safely in Addis Ababa greeting her old friends, hearing Iteffa's painful story, and praying together. In Lusaka, the Strangler was being interrogated by the police, taking them to the spots he had left his victims. He seemed to bask in the attention.

The next day, the tale of the Lusaka Strangler took yet another bizarre turn. While being marched through Central Police Station in handcuffs, he slipped from the assistant superintendent's grasp into a stairwell. He dashed up the stairs and onto the roof of that four-story building with no other way out. He stood on the ledge with police behind him and onlookers below. For over an hour, officials tried to talk him down, but finally he wearied of the exchange and leapt to his death.

Arlene didn't hear the news while she was still in Africa. A few weeks after Arlene was home in Sioux Center, a letter from Leatta arrived with initial rumors about the Strangler but nothing definitive. Leatta had heard a single BBC report that someone had been arrested. Another nurse at the hospital had heard that a friend of hers had helped the police identify the Strangler, but then the Strangler had escaped. Now her friend was afraid the Strangler would come and find her, so she and her husband were leaving the country immediately.

By mid-October, Leatta had not heard anything more about the Strangler. But when one of the young men at the school was acting peculiar, some of the nurses wondered aloud whether he was the Strangler. The Strangler had been alive in their imaginations all those months, and he was still there.

The letter Leatta wrote on Halloween arrived in Sioux Center while Arlene was away on her short deputation trip. On November 19, she returned and read Leatta's news that the season of the Strangler had finally come to an end.

On Monday of Thanksgiving week, Arlene drove the twelve miles to Orange City, eager to hear the X-ray report from Dr. Grossman. He relayed good news: she did not need a biopsy.

As she drove home from the doctor's office on that late November day in 1980, she rejoiced at the beauty of the fields that had been harvested and now lay at rest. She was grateful the threat of cancer was gone. She was grateful she could return to work in Zambia after this furlough. She was grateful the threat of the Lusaka Strangler had ended.

She had no answer as to why such an evil had happened. Why had all those women needlessly lost their lives? Why did Regina's three boys have their mother taken from them? The solution to that mystery died leaping from the roof of the Lusaka Central Police Station. When Arlene returned to her students at Katete, she wouldn't have all the answers to their questions about the season of the Strangler; but she could at least commend the exceptional response of Josephine Mukatasha, who had returned to the scene of the crime, looked for evil, and fought against it.

At the Thanksgiving service at First Reformed Church in Sioux Center, the pastor used the text of Psalm 23 in his sermon. Afterward, Arlene wrote in her journal that she was really blessed by the service and wished she had a tape of it to take with her when she returned to Zambia.

Thank God for love, thank God for faith. There are thorny paths. There are treacherous peaks. Thank God for hope and a cup that overflows.

14

Resignation

Uuvwima tavwimi kamwi.
A hunter does not hunt for one thing.

---

*Phone call from Bruggers. His letter of Nov. 26
said, "You gave them what they needed and wanted
in medical expertise. In a sense they rejected your
understanding of a Christian presence and witness.
Another hospital offers the opportunity to do both."*

December 9, 1980

Through the entirety of Arlene's 1980 furlough, a life-changing question hung in the air: "Should I quit St. Francis?" Although that question was all but answered by the time her furlough began, she was always thorough when it came to seeking God's will for her calling.

Arlene examined the staying-versus-leaving question carefully and from many angles, soliciting the help of several colleagues. Her consideration of the question had begun long before the furlough and even long before she sat down next to Vi Nissley of CMAZ at the Lusaka Assembly of God Church, where Vi told her that the need at Macha was now greater than at Katete. The question had begun before Arlene visited Macha that previous spring and found it so warm and inviting. The question had begun even before Arlene realized that the workload at Katete was not sustainable. The question had begun almost her first week at St. Francis.

Founded as a Christian mission hospital, St. Francis provided a level of healthcare that was severely needed in the region, and its

facilities grew to match the patient demand. Although the administrators remained missionaries, they hired other staff members based
on their medical skills, regardless of their Christian commitment.
By the time Arlene arrived, St. Francis was a mission hospital in
name only. Christianity was tolerated, but a Christian faith was
not expected.

Both Leatta and Arlene were responsible to the mission boards
of their own denominations. They were faithful Christians themselves and held to the Christian vision of their boards. Arlene's
Reformed Church in America (RCA) mission board, like that of
many other churches, understood the importance of interweaving
gospel work with fundamental human needs such as food, shelter,
medicine, and education. Caring for the whole person followed the
model of Jesus. Nevertheless, pursuit of the Great Commission had
always been and continued to be a crucial priority for the Reformed
Church missionary. Arlene was a missionary first, then a nurse, and
then a teacher.

At Katete, Arlene was hired to be a teacher. She was sometimes
required to be a nurse. Her Christian faith was beside the point as
far as St. Francis was concerned.

From Arlene's perspective, she was not at Katete for employment. She was called as a servant of Jesus Christ to go to Katete to
help spread the gospel. That calling was the same for Leatta and
some others on the hospital grounds, like the now ninety-year-old
Father Hewitt. At Katete, Arlene had lived, to the best of her abil-
ity, the life of a missionary; but she did so without the support of a
mission. Arlene's RCA supervisor, Glenn Bruggers, had done his
very best to support her. He had corresponded, visited, and been
both pastoral and protective. However, the efforts of Arlene, Leatta,
Father Hewitt, Glenn, Charles, Partison, Matthew, and others were
not enough to turn this situation into a healthy, Christian mission.

Arlene's question—"Should I quit St. Francis?"—needed to be
formally answered. But she already knew the answer. The real question was when.

There was a woman within the administrative structure of St. Francis who was sort of a bully (we shall call her "B.W.," the "Bully Woman"). B.W. had access to funds through her home country organization. When Dr. Cairns appealed to her for capital expenditures, she could often procure what was needed. This arrangement allowed her certain latitude when her tantrums arose. Since B.W.'s modicum of authority was in the hospital arena, Arlene's tactic was simply to stay out of her way.

It was Arlene's observation that B.W. typically had a single chosen victim. During their first year, B.W. sprayed her venom toward Leatta. Then she switched to another staff member, who ended up not speaking with her for five months. Then Dr. Cairns himself caught her ire. Three times, she resigned and then withdrew her resignation. Later, she went on strike. Shortly after all that, she seemed to forget that anything had happened and began to build a permanent home on the property. But eventually her fangs moved toward Arlene.

At the end of May 1980, a new instructor finally arrived to help the nursing school with its staffing problems. B.W. promptly scheduled shifts in the hospital for the newcomer without notifying Arlene. A small power struggle ensued, and Arlene addressed the issue with Dr. Cairns. When it seemed clear he was not about to go to war with B.W., Arlene's hope for some assistance at the school was shattered. After a two-hour meeting over these matters with Cairns and B.W., Arlene wrote this journal entry:

> *What a waste of time. [B.W.] is using me as a target and scapegoat today. She needs someone to vent her fury on. God, help me to keep from being hurt or angry. I'm really drained. I try to think what facts actually upset me, and there is nothing worth thinking about. Satan uses her to upset others. Cover me with your Blood, Jesus.*

The nothing-worth-thinking-about war between Arlene and B.W. waged from then on, contributing in its small way to the change that was in the wind. Arlene wrote,

Leatta and I feel that [B.W.] is Evil and probably the major problem of Katete. She has switched to her "little girl" act.

This was a voice and attitude Arlene had observed on several occasions. B.W. would smile, adopt a sweet voice, and cock her head, trusting she would thereby achieve acquiescence. If that didn't work, what followed was raging volume and coarse speech. If that didn't work, there were proclamations that she would have the person "removed from this hospital!" If that didn't work, she resigned. Although B.W. was good at manipulations, she wasn't so good at her actual job. Leatta did a fair amount of coming along behind her, cleaning up after her ineptitude. By mid-1980, Leatta was pushed over the edge and began calculating her own date of departure from St. Francis. Leatta's pending resignation concerned Arlene a great deal, because she was counting on Leatta to cover for her when she went on furlough that fall.

Then Arlene began praying for B.W. in earnest, following the advice of Jeremiah 29:7: "But seek the welfare of the city where I have sent you into exile, and pray to the LORD on its behalf, for in its welfare you will find your welfare." She wrote in her journal,

We need to pray for our "oppressors." Guard against self-pity and resentment.

The anxiety of this season was caused not only by B.W. and the lost Christian vision of St. Francis's missionary founders. It was also compounded by an inadequate supply of basic necessities in that region of the world. For example, there had been no soap in the stores for nearly two years. "To go shopping" was no longer defined as "selecting items for purchase." A shopping trip was a matter of seeing what was on the shelves and buying whatever was available that could reasonably be useful in the foreseeable future.

One beautiful Saturday in June, Arlene drove over to Chipata to Adams General Supplies. She was thrilled to find powdered milk, evaporated milk, condensed milk, sugar, iodized salt, and, yes, soap! She bought all she could afford, and then she attended a garden show. It was a day of "deep, sweet peace of mind and heart."

A week later, all that "sweet peace" was gone when Arlene had to adjust the times of her lectures to attend a specially called administrative meeting. At this meeting, B.W. demanded that certain nurses be removed from their teaching duties and reassigned to the hospital. Knowing that such an arrangement would prevent her furlough, Arlene felt heartsick. She wanted to work in a place where the staff at least aspired to follow the apostle Paul's commendation: "Love each other with genuine affection. Take delight in honoring each other" (Romans 12:10 NLT). She was not accustomed to fighting for her rights in a mission institution—this had not been her experience in either the Sudan or in Ethiopia. Scheming and manipulation were of no interest to her.

It was in this state of mind that Arlene went to Lusaka for GNC meetings and sat next to Vi Nissley at church, and heard how she was needed as the tutor in Macha.

When Arlene returned to St. Francis, she learned that Leatta had decided to resign by the following June. She could no longer take B.W., the heavy workload, and the loss of her missionary calling. Arlene knew how she felt. After their long talk that night, Arlene sat down to write a first draft of her own resignation letter.

Leatta wrote to her mission board, describing the situation as "difficult and indescribable." She told her supervisor that the mission itself had become a mission field. Though her contract was due for renewal that fall, she was willing to stay so Arlene could go on furlough. After covering that leave, she would leave as soon as a transition could be arranged.

For her part, Arlene articulated her concerns to her own supervisor, Glenn, but with a caveat: "I certainly do not feel like I ought to leave a difficult place of service unless I know for sure that God is leading me to work elsewhere."

On her next GNC trip to Lusaka, Arlene stopped at the office of Churches Medical Association of Zambia. While there, she learned the welcome news that a nursing instructor had applied and was being considered for Katete. She was British, Anglican, forty-eight, and experienced, having taught nursing for ten years. This woman seemed an appropriate fit to replace Arlene if she transferred to Macha. Arlene took it as a good indication that the timing might be right if she was wanted at Macha. She then learned that Macha would be delighted to receive her immediately following her furlough. Arlene appealed to the Lord for his direction and spoke to everyone else involved.

While she was still in Lusaka, she went to the Examination Committee that graded the final exams of St. Francis's Set 54, the students who had started two years earlier at the same time as Arlene. Much to her delight, they all passed, and two of them even passed with honors. Perhaps, she thought, her goal of raised standards was bearing fruit.

She looked forward to letting the students know how well they had all done, but she would have to remain silent for two weeks until the official letter from GNC made its way to Katete.

Arlene knew that Tuesdays were the days Dr. Cairns set aside for administrative tasks. That day would be the best to broach the subject of a potential change. On a Tuesday afternoon in mid-August, Arlene and Leatta invited James and Faith Cairns for 5:00 tea. After the tea was poured and cookies were served, Arlene got to her point. Leatta was content for Arlene to relay both of their stories.

"Before I leave on furlough in a few weeks, I felt it was important to begin a conversation about my possible transfer. And Leatta will factor in here as well. She knows about this, so—"

"You're worrying me," Faith interrupted.

"Let her speak, Love," said Dr. Cairns.

Arlene then laid it out as succinctly as she could. She reminded them she had been recruited for Macha before Katete. She told about encountering Vi Nissley at church and how Vi had shared the present need in Macha. Arlene also revealed that she knew about the possible arrival of a new instructor for St. Francis. "With a new sister instructor arriving, I won't be leaving you in the lurch."

Faith asked, "How does Leatta factor into all this?"

Arlene went forward gently but boldly: "It should come as no surprise to you that [B.W.'s] attitude is difficult. That has fallen heavily on Leatta in the past, and now it falls on me. We no longer want to work with her."

Faith was stunned. "Are you saying it's her or you, and we have to choose?"

Arlene shook her head. "No. We're saying that we came here expecting to work at a mission. That assumes a common set of values. And those values are not always evident . . . here."

Leatta spoke up. "My contract was for two years. I'll stay through Arlene's furlough, and then, well, we can arrange a good time for me to go. But I can't stay. That's not a threat. I've decided, regardless."

Faith asked, "And you, Arlene? Have you definitely decided?"

"No. I work primarily for my mission board, so I need to have conversations with them, which should happen while I'm on furlough. But there's also impact for you, and CMAZ, and the people at Macha. I'm just starting a conversation over what's best for all concerned." After a pause, Arlene continued, "And frankly, Leatta has been . . . well, without her, it will be very difficult for me to continue here." Then Arlene laughed. "I'm not afraid of difficult. A person wouldn't come here at all if comfort was the goal."

Dr. Cairns said gravely, "I cannot accept your reasoning unless you can declare with certainty that this is God's plan for you."

Arlene was stunned. It was the first time he had ever insisted that she or anyone else on the hospital grounds seek God's will or even affirm the Christian faith. His response seemed out of character and therefore manipulative; it appeared as if he was using her own faith against hr. But then she realized that she agreed with him. Completely. She would transfer only if it was God's will for her. And she could not yet, with certainty, declare that such was the case.

With exasperation, he went on: "I only agreed to go to all the effort to recruit another tutor because you begged me to, and now you're telling me that you had an ulterior motive of using her to replace you? I know they have needs at Macha. Wouldn't it have been easier to let the new tutor go there?!"

Faith threw a bunch of stuff at the wall to see if any of it would stick. "We don't even know this new tutor. What is she like? Will she fit here? You've done all the work to improve St. Francis. Are you willing to just up and leave it? And if you turn it over to somebody new who none of us know about, it may fall down flat. Is that what you want? I should think not."

"Of course not—"

Dr. Cairns held up a hand for calm and said, "Look—"

But Faith rushed on. "You're terribly tired. This is no time to be making any long-term decisions. Let's all give it a rest." Then she seemed excited about an idea she had. "Here's what you should do. You should go for a visit to Macha once more and see it with a fresh eye. For all you know, you'd be going from a frying pan into a fire, and none of us wants that for you."

Dr. Cairns laid a hand on his wife's arm. "Arlene, go and have your furlough. Leatta will hold down the fort here. But please commit to staying at least six months after." There was a pause and then he asked, "Can we all agree?"

Arlene was not about to make sudden commitments, but she could agree to something. "I've experienced what it was like to arrive with no one here and things in disarray. I assure you that I will not leave without a proper turnover to whoever is the new—"

"Principal tutor," Dr. Cairns finished her sentence.

"Yes, that," said Arlene, though she had never liked the term. It seemed too pretentious.

Arlene knew she wouldn't have time to visit Macha prior to her furlough. Besides, it was not a matter of seeing the grounds at Macha. It was a matter of mission, and she was already convinced that the Macha Mission Hospital was, well, a mission. They had asked for her statement of faith at the start of their process. No such question had been asked by St. Francis. Indeed, her recommendations had been requested only after she was already appointed.

The next day, August 13, her beloved Josh fell sick. He didn't eat. He was listless, and his breathing grew labored. Arlene tied him up so she could keep an eye on him. Normally, he would have struggled if she tried to attach a leash, but he just lay there. His listlessness continued for the next two days, and Arlene wrote in her journal, "I don't want to lose him. He is a good watch dog and a friend to me."

At Arlene's request, the vet came to have a look. His diagnosis was tick fever, and he gave Josh a shot of aureomycin. No improvement. A friend suggested to Arlene that she should untie him since he might think he was being punished. She took that advice, and he just lay there for another day. The vet returned three days in a row to give Josh more shots. Finally, after eight days, he took a bone in his mouth and began moving a bit.

The day after Josh began to get better, the official final exam results for Set 54 arrived. Arlene sent word for the entire Set to meet her in the school library. The savviest students would have calculated the good news: when not everyone passed, she met with each student one at a time. The final examination announcements were always a cause for great joy or great sorrow, because the entire previous two years of their lives hung on that moment.

Arlene smiled and cut to the chase: "Everyone passed!"

The shouting could be heard across the grounds at the hospital. The leaping, hugging, and crying continued until Arlene raised her hand. When they were quiet, she continued. "Sebah and Roydah passed with honors!" And the bedlam began all over again.

Gone on a five-day excursion to the Luangwa Game Park, the Cairns stopped back at St. Francis on their way through to the remaining twelve days of their vacation over at Lake Malawi.

Before leaving for Malawi, Dr. Cairns stopped by to tell Arlene something. As he turned to leave her office, he attempted to encourage her. "Oh, before I go, I've been thinking about your Macha situation. The decision will have to be yours, of course. You are clearly wanted in two places at once, and, of course, it is not possible to divide you in half. If you leave, our school will be short-handed again after all our work to remedy that—especially since we don't know how the new tutor will fit in and adjust and so forth. If you do want to transfer to Macha, you'll want to be there well before the new intake of students. You'll remember from when you started how difficult that transition can be."

"Yes. I arrived the day before Set 54 began."

"So, you wouldn't want to repeat that. But I definitely wouldn't want you to leave here before—"

Arlene interjected some encouragement of her own. "The new principal tutor is coming from England and is Anglican. She'll have no adjustment to the British way. She's experienced, but younger than I, so—"

"So, you've definitely decided then?"

"No, that's not . . . that's not what I meant. I'll still need to discuss things with my supervisor and mission board."

"Well, yes, of course. Them. Yes."

"And I really am exhausted. Best not to make important decisions under such circumstances."

"Righto. You need to take some rest."

Then the old argument heated up again as Arlene tried to make her case. "The system here with scheduling students for the wards requires each block to be taught twice. If that system is to be continued, you must have at least five instructors. The government has mandated it, I've affirmed it repeatedly, and you—"

"I don't disagree! But how can I maintain a roster if my tutors quit on me just when things are coming into shape?!"

Arlene did not answer.

"Never mind," said Dr. Cairns. "That's why I get the administrator salary."

And that's why, thought Arlene, you get to go on vacation.

The graduation for Set 54 took place while the Cairns were away. Arlene baked two orange breads, and Mrs. Mzamo made the cakes. The school was packed, and the drumming began as the graduates entered. Set 57 sang, in anticipation of the day when they would come marching in. That night, Arlene wrote this reflection:

Two years ago I wondered how I would get through two years when I saw the mess I was entering here. Nothing in order in the school office. The hopeless shortage of staff and the demanding schedule. At the end of two years, I see what a price there has been to pay—physically, emotionally, mentally. The new offer to go to

Macha may well be the Lord directing me elsewhere. The upcoming furlough will help me get a better perspective. My tiredness makes it hard to make a right decision. "Have mercy on me, O God, according to thy lovingkindness, according to the multitude of thy tender mercies blot out my transgressions" (Ps. 51:1).

By the end of her furlough, Arlene was offered a three-year term of service at the Macha Mission Hospital as the tutor. Although she had completed an application form in 1978, they asked for her to fill out another form of information that included the question, "What do Christ and the Christian faith mean to you?"

Arlene wrote a short testimony:

Jesus Christ is the Son of God who died for my sins. He has done so much for me. As my Shepherd he leads and guides me, and it is my desire to follow where he leads me. I want to be His disciple and by word and action seek to introduce others to Him. My Christian faith is the most precious possession. I'm sorry that it is still so weak and I do not trust Him as fully as I should.

At the end of February 1981, St. Francis gathered for a ceremony to say goodbye to their departing principal tutor. The senior hospital staff was present, including B.W., who wore her favorite scowl. As a going-away gift, they presented Arlene with a book about the Luangwa Game Park, a place she never had the time to see for herself.

15

Water

Chaakanza mulonga musena.
A river is created by rivulets.

Up early. This is the day. Don got Josh in the car
without much trouble and I was off at 7:00 a.m. Last
40 miles very rough took 2 hours. A Zambian boy,
Elijah, rode with me. Several stopped in to welcome me.
It will take time to get settled. Father, help me take one
day at a time and rest in You.

March 3, 1981

Arlene's first months in Macha flew by. She was learning a new school, new community, new tribal group (the Tonga), and new church subculture (the Brethren in Christ). In early August, the Brethren in Christ churches of Zimbabwe and Zambia gathered at Macha for their annual General Conference.

On Sunday morning, the final day of General Conference of 1981, Arlene arrived at the church on Sunday morning shortly before 8:00. The temperature that early was chilly, in the 50s. An August day in southwest Zambia would almost without fail rise into the high 70s, and there would be no rain. But at this time of day, Arlene wore a sweater over her blouse. She also wore a calf-length *chitenge* to cover her legs. Her feet were donned with sandals but no stockings. She carried her Bible and journal.

Macha was the chosen site of this year's conference because it was the seventy-fifth anniversary of the founding of the mission.

Yesterday, the Zambian prime minister had made the arduous trek to this rural institution to bring greetings and witness the historical pageant of the two women who arrived by oxcart to seek permission from Chief Macha to start a school. His son was their first student.

The focus of today's itinerary was totally on Jesus. Arlene had arrived early as she did not want to miss the planned event: at age fifty-eight, she had never experienced the ritual of foot washing. The service began inside the crowded church building with a sermon on humility (which Arlene described as "vivid and touching, one that I'll probably always remember") by Dr. Kurien, a doctor from India who was on staff at the hospital. His text was John 13:4-5.

> So during the meal Jesus got up, removed his outer garment, and wrapped a towel around his waist. He put some water into a large bowl. Then he began washing his disciples' feet and drying them with the towel he was wearing. [CEV].

After the sermon, the men and boys—who had been seated as usual on the left side of the sanctuary—stood up and went outside. The women and girls stayed inside and arranged the chairs into circles of twelve throughout the room. There were about ten deaconesses who served and coordinated the groups, bringing each a basin of water and a large towel. One woman in each group then stood and tied the towel around her waist. Holding the basin, she knelt in front of the woman next to her.

It was an African woman who knelt in front of Arlene. Arlene had never met her before. Setting the basin directly in front of Arlene, the woman reached forward to unlatch one of Arlene's sandals and take it off. She held Arlene's foot above the basin and dipped the other hand to carry water to the foot, rubbing the water over the foot, then drying the foot with the towel, and tenderly replacing the sandal without letting the foot touch the floor. She repeated the gesture with Arlene's other foot. The point was not a physical washing. Indeed, participants had taken special care to wash their own feet in preparation for the day. Just as the bread and cup of their upcoming Communion service were for spiritual rather than physical sustenance, the water on the feet was a promise of service toward God and one another.

By now, someone had started singing a familiar hymn from memory and others had joined in. When the woman finished washing both of Arlene's feet, she stood and reached a hand forward to shake Arlene's hand. When Arlene took her hand, the woman gently pulled Arlene to her feet and embraced her. Then she kissed her on the cheek, removed the towel, and handed it to Arlene. Arlene tied it around her waist and knelt in front of the next woman in the circle, Lois Thuma, a member of the extended family of Alvan and Ardys Thuma, founders of the Macha hospital.

The songs flowed easily from one to the next. No words were spoken. Arlene later called it "unhurried and lovely."

When each woman had been served by another, the basins and towels were taken away, and the chairs were put back in rows. Someone went outside to tell the men that they could return when their own foot washing service was completed. When all were assembled, the Communion service was held.

The entire morning was new and familiar—all at the same time. She felt at home.

In addition to her delight with the Christian fellowship at Macha, Arlene enjoyed the beautiful weather. She planted a poinsettia hedge and a garden, which she watered faithfully since no significant rain was expected until November.

Although the weather across Zambia is pretty much the same, the plateau at Macha rests at a considerably lower altitude than Katete. Arlene was warned it could get hotter here than she had experienced over at St. Francis or up on Lusaka's higher plateau. The temperature at Macha could easily rise above 100 degrees Fahrenheit; when combined with humidity, it might be oppressive and wearisome. Arlene, however, remembered the Sudan. She was prepared.

Besides being much hotter, Macha was also more remote than Katete. The distance from the capital city out to Macha was only 220 miles compared with the 300 miles between Lusaka and Katete. But the trip to Macha, although it was shorter, took longer because of the dirt roads for the last forty miles. In 1906, Chief Macha had approved this location for the mission, not for its proximity to a city but because it was the center of his people and their farms. The Macha mission was truly and intentionally out in the bush.

Sometimes the infrastructure lagged behind the need. As the school and hospital had grown, the need for water had grown as well. By the time Arlene arrived at Macha, the mission hospital had 208 beds, 57 nursing students, 243 high school girls, plus all the support staff and the family members who camped nearby to care for their loved ones being treated in the hospital.

Water access was largely dependent on a reservoir the locals called "the Dam," which was a pond that had been created by damming a nearby stream. Water was pumped from the Dam to a water tower on the mission grounds. Although Dam water required additional filtering by individuals, it sustained the community while they waited for rain each year.

The dry season began in April, but the weather then was pleasant and sometimes even cool. The summer months were delightful. But Arlene's first Macha hot season arrived with a sudden blast the last week of August, even earlier than usual. Arlene noted in her journal that the temperature was in the 90s, creeping higher day by day accompanied by thickening humidity. There were no fans in the buildings and little movement of air. Thankfully, the temperatures fell some in the nights, so she had no trouble sleeping. Not yet.

Back in Katete, Arlene had heard October called "suicide month" because of the unremitting heat. That term seemed even more fitting in Macha where she recorded that at the start of the month it was 95 in the shade.

Arlene learned that it might rain in October, but an October rain is not the start of the rainy season. The occasional October rain is called "that which saves the cattle," because a small amount of rain can provide enough green shoots of grass to sustain the cows until November. Nevertheless, October in southwest Zambia often threatens to be a scorching and miserable month.

By mid-October, Arlene was getting up at 4:00 because the early morning was the only time she felt it was cool enough to function productively. She continued serving on the GNC, a role that meant traveling two or even three times a month into Lusaka where it was cooler, rain fell more often, and sometimes fans or even air conditioning brought relief.

Out at Macha during Arlene's first so-called rainy season, the rain was sadly sparse and the temperatures remained unusually high. Whereas forty inches of rain were expected, only fourteen inches fell that year. Everyone at the mission was grateful for the Dam, but its water level dropped lower and lower—an ominous precursor to the oncoming drought of 1982.

Macha's rainy season of 1982 was indeed just as unusually hot and dry as the previous year. On November 4, Arlene recorded the temperature as 104 degrees at midday. A week later, the mission staff had a planning meeting about water. It was confirmed that the Dam was dry, and the back-up borehole was likewise dangerously unproductive. There was to be no more watering of gardens or taking of showers.

The backup plan was expensive, but at least there was a plan. Tanker trucks were hired out of Choma to drive back and forth, pumping water out of swamps thirty miles away. The muddy water was pumped into the mission water tower from as many as eight truckloads a day.

By early December, nothing more than a light rain had fallen and the borehole also dried up. The combination of heat and stress made it difficult for Arlene to sleep at night or function well in the day. Some of her colleagues admitted to being depressed. Of course, the stress was not theirs alone but belonged to the entire region. Every day was expected to be the last day of the dry season. Every sprinkle raised hopes that melted in the midday heat. Arlene set out pails to catch water off the roof in case some rain did fall. She used it to wash only enough clothes to wear, and leftover cleaning water was used to flush the toilet.

On one of her visits to Lusaka, Arlene found a Philips desktop electric fan on sale. It was ridiculously expensive at 250 kwacha, about $330 U.S. She bought it. She drove home in heavy rain, wondering if she had just made a foolish purchase since it was possible the rainy season had finally begun. About ten miles from Macha, the sky cleared. There had not been enough rain in Macha to even settle the dust.

"Come and see! Come and see!"

Arlene didn't feel like going outside under the blazing hot sun. She wondered what was so important.

"You have to see this with your own eyes! Come and see."

She wasn't the kind of teacher inclined to give up precious class time, but she and her students noticed considerable activity outside their classroom windows. Arlene called out to someone in the yard, "Where is everyone going?"

"To the Dam! To the Dam!"

"Let's go," she said. And everyone who was able ran to the Dam.

Dark clouds surrounded Macha. Rain seemed to be falling all around but not here. When they arrived at the Dam, there was already some water in it, and as the Macha crowd watched, the level steadily rose. "Gushing!" was a word someone used. Rainfall in the surrounding catchment area was filling the tributaries and finding its way downhill to the Macha Dam. By the end of the afternoon, water was spilling over the Dam. Later that same week, rain fell in Macha itself. Arlene journaled,

Raining off and on all day—the real rainy season kind. So grateful. Temperature dropped to 80 degrees. It feels so cool.

There was only a month or so left in the rainy season, so it wasn't likely this year would produce the expected and needed amount of forty inches. But the community was deeply grateful for what had arrived.

On Sunday, a group from the church took another walk to the Dam, picking up large stones on the way. Someone brought along cement, and they gathered fifty feet from the water's edge. Someone read from Joshua 4, one of the several biblical stories when God made water do something surprising. After the Joshua 4 miracle, the people of Israel took stones and set them up as a memorial. Joshua commanded the people that when future generations asked what the stones meant they were to tell the story of God's provision.

After the reading of that Scripture, one by one the Macha people piled their stones and cemented them together. It was a rustic pile, formed by young and old at the edge of the Macha Dam, designed to merge the miracle of 1982 to the ancient stories. In the future, when someone asked the meaning of this heap of stones, it could be told how God provided water for the people of Macha.

Those stones are there to this day.

On January 30, 1983, Arlene wrote this letter:

Dear friends in my Home Church:

Greetings to all of you on this gorgeous cool (85 degree) Sunday morning at 8:45 with bird songs in the background and the windows wide open to catch a few early morning breezes!

The most wonderful news all of us from Macha have at the moment is that we had six inches of rain the past week! It rained days and nights in the most gentle rain you can imagine and all of nature, including us, just soaked it in. We finally realized that it was no longer necessary to put out all the pails and basins to catch as much as possible. Hesitatingly we put water in the bathtub for it seemed like we were wasting it to use so much water for just a bath! I guess we will always turn off the spigot between wetting the tooth brush instead of just letting it run. The toilet can be flushed as necessary and not limited to once a day with waste water. I still wash dishes once a day in a basin rather than in the sink and save the glass of water which I didn't empty when having a drink. We still need a lot before we reach the annual quota of 40 inches, but we are so grateful to God and may we never take even a glassful of water for granted. We must use this precious gift of God more sparingly and conservatively. Praise God for water!

Later that year, Arlene's church took a special offering. They sent $15,541.94 for a new, deeper well. The money was used to dig a well and install pipes and a pump. There was enough money left over to purchase one ton of milk for the region's malnourished children. Powdered milk. Just add water.

16

Graduation

Kufwa muntu zina talibundi.
A person dies but the name remains.

Teaching—preparing for graduation—busy preparing program. My blood pressure up I think. Big feast for Dr. Kurien. Very large crowd. Butcher gave a calf. Everyone invited. Practice at night.

July 23, 1982

The final exams of Macha Nurses Training School Set 23 had been graded and the scores announced and either rejoiced over or bemoaned. Now the weekend had arrived for the solemn celebration. Since Arlene's transfer to the Zambian rural west, this would be her third Set to graduate. Twenty-three cohorts of Zambian Enrolled Nursing students had matriculated through the school in its dozen or so years of existence.

The day before graduation was for feasting and fellowship. As Arlene finished supper and walked over to the church building for rehearsal, seven times zones earlier in Sioux Center, Iowa, Arlene's mother lay in bed suffering with pneumonia. Her hacking cough, sleeplessness, and difficulty breathing had reached a point of great concern. Her weakness made it difficult to get her up out of bed, which also made it difficult for her family to provide the care she needed. Grada, Harriet, and Bernice (the three of Ma's six daughters who lived in Sioux County) agreed to add their mother's name to the waiting list for "the Wing," a long-term care section of the local hospital. If Ma improved, then they would withdraw her name. But for now, they needed to get her on the list as she might soon need a level of care they were unequipped to give.

In the midst of this uncertain time, Grada took a much-needed break to visit her youngest sister, Milly, in western Michigan. At midday on Friday, July 23, Grada called home to ask Bernice how things were going.

Bernice reported, "Well, it's hot here! Is it hot there?"

"It's warm, but we have the lake effect. Not as bad as there, I'm sure. How's Ma doing?"

"Well, we have a quandary. The Nursing Wing called. They suddenly have a room available. I'm sure she wouldn't want it. But do we want it?"

"Already? That was fast."

"I thought it would be months before we had to decide."

Grada paused and then said, "Well, it was . . . I think it might have been . . ." She sighed and spilled the beans. "Before I left for Michigan, I just happened to tell our neighbor that we put Ma's name in for the Wing. And he said he was on the hospital board."

"He said he was on the hospital board?"

"He said he was on the hospital board."

"What did he mean by that?" asked Bernice.

"What do you think he meant?"

"Do you think he pulled some strings?"

"They think the world of Ma."

"Ma wouldn't want special treatment to get in," said Bernice. "Should I tell them no thank you?"

"Please tell them we'll take it," Grada responded.

"We'll take it?"

"She needs help. If she gets better, she can move home."

"All right, we'll try."

"Milly is taking me out in the boat tomorrow," said Grada. "But I'll call in the evening."

Bernice telephoned the Wing and said they would take the room.

The question now was how to get Ma there. If they called an ambulance, the price was $50.00, and Ma would have a conniption. Instead, Harriet came to town to help. The two daughters transferred Ma from her bed to her wheelchair. Out on the driveway, their husbands easily lifted Ma in her wheelchair—less than a hundred pounds total—into the back of one of their pickup trucks. The daughters sat with Ma in the bed of the truck, cooing over her on their slow roll to the Wing. If you had been driving down Highway 75 through Sioux Center that Friday afternoon, you would have seen a pickup crossing from the east, carrying an elderly lady in her royal carriage, surrounded by her pages. It was safe—and it was free.

At the Wing, Bernice was appalled by the heat. There was no air-conditioning, but there was a window. Bernice announced she would go hunting for a window air conditioner, even if she had to make the hour drive to Sioux City. Harriet sat with Ma for a time, and then excused herself to take a break and check on her kids, leaving Ma alone.

The nurse's aide came into the room to feed Ma an early supper. The eldest daughter, Harriet, was feeding her own family. Arlene, daughter number two, had gone to bed in Zambia, resting up for Saturday's graduation ceremony. Bernice was on her way from Sioux City with a new air conditioner in tow. Joyce was in Wisconsin at the church parsonage, where she lived with her pastor husband. Grada and Milly were at the lake. This supper would turn out to be Ma's last. The aide could not have known the extent of Ma's swallowing problem. It's believed she choked on her food, slipping away after the aide left the room.

She never wanted to spend even a night in the Wing. As it turned out, she was granted her wish, sailing toward heaven in the back of that pickup truck.

The next morning was the Zambian Enrolled Nurses graduation. Arlene rose especially early, had a good breakfast, and was in her office by 7:00 a.m. She was gathering the programs and diplomas when she heard a timid knock at the door. It was Ali, one of the staff nurses. She was there to deliver a message that had been cabled to Choma and transferred to Macha:

ARLENE SCHUITEMAN'S MOTHER HAS PASSED AWAY.

The grief hit suddenly and strong. She struggled to remain on her feet. She of course immediately understood this news was an answer to her prayers that Ma would be set free from her earthly imprisonment. Nevertheless, Arlene fought for air. When she could speak, she wanted to know the details, but Ali had nothing more to offer. The nearest telephone was two hours up the Choma road. Arlene covered her mouth and turned away. Ali fiddled with the keys on the desk and then excused herself, absent-mindedly taking Arlene's key ring, and locking the office door behind her. It was a dead bolt lock. Without her keys, Arlene was imprisoned in her office.

Hearing the click of the lock, Arlene turned to the door.

"Ali?" No answer. What was the meaning of this? Arlene went to the window to see Ali trotting quickly back to the hospital.

"Ali!" Arlene rapped on the window. Ali became smaller and then disappeared. Arlene rapped again. Surely someone would hear. But it was early Saturday morning.

"Help."

No one.

"Help! I'm locked in here!"

Nothing.

She suddenly felt so very alone, so far away from Ma, Pa, and the farmhouse where she and her sisters had all been born. She could remember the births of her youngest sisters—Ma laboring in the first-floor bedroom on the east side of the house. After each birth, Pa had gone out into the pasture and dug a hole. Arlene had not known what he was doing or known enough to even ask. It was only much later that she learned he was following an ancient Dutch tradition: the burying of a child's umbilical cord, which anchored each of his girls to the farm, to their family, and to their home. Arlene wept and shouted and then wept some more. Eventually composing herself, she slid open the window and crawled up onto the window sill.

On graduation morning in July 1982 in Macha, Zambia, you could have seen the brown lace-up shoes and stockings of the standard Zambian nurse's uniform extending awkwardly out an office window before the head tutor herself shimmied through and tumbled to the ground.

Graduation, under Arlene's leadership, was a big deal. This milestone celebrated a significant journey and a noted accomplishment. A thousand students had applied for Macha's Set 23, and only 7 percent of those applicants had been invited to take an entrance exam and sit for an interview. Twelve of seventy interviewees were selected for Set 23, and of those twelve, ten made it to graduation.

Graduation day celebrated an achievement for the students, the school, and the whole mission. Zambia's goal of "Health for all by the year 2000" held out special hope for rural areas such as the Macha catchment which served a population of 160,000. Each new cohort of medical professionals was a needed step forward.

For all these reasons, and to encourage the upcoming Sets, Arlene did all she could to mark graduation day. Each year she invited dignitaries, and today's graduation was attended by Mr. Nyanga, a member of the national parliament.

Arlene put on her best face, but by the time Mr. Nyanga rose to address the assembly, he had learned of Arlene's loss. After the applause for Mr. Nyanga had subsided, he asked everyone to rise to their feet and then said, "The mother of Sister Schuiteman has passed away. I ask that we all stand in silence to remember the Schuiteman family."

Everyone bowed their heads, and Arlene bit her lip.

That afternoon, Ali accompanied Arlene to the telephone in the city. Arlene wanted more details about what had happened, and she needed to hear her sisters' voices. By 2:00 p.m., the blue Datsun was on the Choma road. The trip was especially bone-jarring since Arlene drove the dusty washboard as fast as safety permitted. At 9:00 a.m. Iowa time, Bernice picked up the phone at the farm and heard a voice from Zambia. Bernice then related the details of the day before, the mysterious leap to the top of the waiting list, the unusual ambulance ride, and the new air conditioner that Bernice now planned to return. Arlene also learned of Ma's final breaths, as much as could be known.

The only other sister Arlene was able to reach by phone from Choma was Joyce in Wisconsin. She confirmed that all the sisters were waiting on Arlene: Was she planning to come home? Should they delay the funeral plans? Since Arlene had no certainty of getting a ticket or even of a ride to the Lusaka airport, she had to make a decision that broke her heart. "Go ahead without me," she said. Although Arlene had missed so many events, this was the most painful of all. She hung up the phone and cried all the way back to Macha.

That evening, several friends gathered in Arlene's living room, encouraging her to go home for the funeral, even offering to cover Arlene's classes for several weeks. Dr. Spurrier encouraged her to at least try and go. The hospital van had a scheduled trip to Lusaka at 8:00 a.m., and once in Lusaka, she could telephone the airport or even go there to inquire about a last-minute reservation or standby. They would loan her whatever money she needed. At 10:30 p.m., Arlene said yes, she would try to make the trip.

She slept for two hours. Then she got up and wrote some letters and instructions for her possible absence. She collected all the documents required for travel between countries: passport, work permit, tax clearance, reentry papers, and proof of vaccinations. At the appointed time of departure, she joined the small crowd standing by the van.

Typically, when the mission's Toyota van headed into the capital city, potential passengers announced their hope to get a place on board. They might have reasons of business or recreation in Lusaka. They might have a long-planned need or a sudden need, as in Arlene's case. There might be an entire family traveling, as was the case that morning. Dr. Kurien's family was traveling back to India. He was the doctor who had preached the foot-washing day sermon that was so vivid and touching that Arlene felt she would remember it all her life. Luggage was piled in the back of the van, leaving room under the seats and in the top carrier for groceries and supplies that would be packed on the return trip to the mission later that week.

Arlene was grateful to have a seat in the van and room for her luggage. She hoped, however, that she wouldn't need a seat on that week's return trip. Her goal was to purchase tickets on a series of connecting flights that would bring her to where her family could pick her up and transport her the rest of the way. Although the plan was full of uncertainties, she needed at least to try to return home in time for her mother's funeral.

The coolness of the night wore off quickly in the stuffiness of the vehicle, so the windows were opened to let in some freshness. In came a blast of heat, dust, and noise. Since a little moving air was worth the negative side effects, the windows stayed open as the van vibrated along the country road, struggling to reach the main highway as quickly and safely as possible. Arlene was grateful the conditions mitigated against conversation. She was not in the mood to talk.

A man named Kayumba had brought along a transistor radio, and he thought that music might be a balm to Arlene's troubled spirit. He fussed with the dial until he found the Voice of South Africa. He could not have found a more perfect song for Arlene that morning than the Fanny Crosby hymn that came wafting in from the southern tip of the continent: "Safe in the Arms of Jesus." The lyrics would have been tricky to discern in that noisy van if Arlene had not sung them from memory since her childhood:

> Safe in the arms of Jesus, safe on His gentle breast,
> There by His love o'ershaded, sweetly my soul shall rest.
> Hark! 'tis the voice of angels, borne in a song to me.
> Over the fields of glory, over the jasper sea.

Arlene imagined her mother's new experience—a land where Ma could sing again, joining the angelic song, wading through yellow pastures and walking across the sea of glass to the throne of heaven.

The lyrics were an assurance of her mother's new life, as well as a reminder that Arlene herself would wait through "only a few more trials, only a few more tears."

> Jesus, my heart's dear Refuge, Jesus has died for me;
> Firm on the Rock of Ages, ever my trust shall be.
> Here let me wait with patience, wait till the night is over;
> Wait till I see the morning break on the golden shore.

Iowa and Africa, earth and heaven, sorrow and hope harmonized in a Toyota van that turned the corner from the Monze road onto the Line of Rail toward Lusaka on that last Sunday morning of July 1982.

The trip took unusually long. They had two flats on the way—which Arlene barely noticed, lost in thought. In the city, Chet Sollenberger's wife Milly gave Arlene something to eat while Chet sought information on flights. In short order, Arlene was booked to fly out that very night, the expense paid on Chet's credit card. He handed her the card and said, "Use it to get yourself home and back."

As Arlene's plane approached London, morning light splashed across the clouds, turning them golden. Arlene described the moment in her journal:

> *The sunrise so gorgeous . . . and I thought of Mom as free at last—to see, to taste, to smell, to walk and run—I just wonder how in her sweet, humble, and surprised way she is experiencing the fullness of joy. Oh God, what a blessing. Thank you.*

Shortly before her flight took off from Heathrow, she could wait no longer, even though she knew it was only 5:00 a.m. in Sioux Center. Grada picked up the call and let her know that the funeral was taking place at 10:30 that morning. Arlene said she understood and that she would land in Sioux Falls that evening.

So that Arlene could see her mother one last time, her sisters had not yet laid Ma's body to rest next to Pa's in the cemetery near First Reformed Church. On Tuesday morning, Arlene slipped over to the chapel to view her mother in her coffin, attired in her best flowered dress with white gloves.

It was remarkable that only four days after hearing of her mother's death, Arlene was home in Iowa to pay her final respects. She watched as one of the undertakers removed Ma's glasses and lowered the lid on the casket in preparation for transfer via the hearse to the cemetery, where the backhoe had already dug the grave and installed the concrete liner.

Arlene compared these customs to the first funeral she had witnessed at Macha. She and a small band of church members had traveled to a neighboring village to worship with a gathering of fellow Christians. When they arrived at the village, no one was there except one woman who told them that everyone had gone to a funeral in the next village. The funeral was easy to find, as they only needed to follow the sound of wailing.

Inside a small hut lay the body of a child who had died in the night. The family's three wives held vigil and wailed, while the father and a few helpers built a coffin in the yard. Other men were busy a short walk away, digging in the hard, dry ground with pickaxes and shovels. Every so often, a newcomer who had just heard the terrible news came running, at which point the weeping and wailing rose in volume. When all was ready, the coffin was solemnly carried into the hut. As Arlene sat under a tree, she heard the tap, tap, tap of one nail after another, and the weeping grew more sorrowful yet. Four men carried the small coffin out of the hut and down the path into the tall grass. The two wives whose child had not died carried large pails of water on their heads. Everyone followed.

The coffin was laid next to the fresh hole. The pastor led some songs and prayers. Scripture was read and a short sermon was spoken. Then the father rose and thanked everyone for coming. The coffin was lowered into the grave. The father was handed a white, plastic cup. He pierced it with a spear and placed it into the grave, and the men mounded the earth back into the hole. The buckets of water were brought near, and the water was poured over the men's hands, spilling on to the fresh mound so that all the earth taken from the grave would be returned to the grave. An old woman came forward and sprinkled the last of the water onto the mound. Ten women came forward and patted the grave site with their hands Then the child's grandmother sang the song heard all over the earth: "Why am I left instead of this little child?"

The Sunday following Ma's interment, Arlene was asked to share a few words during worship. She told this story:

Adeline, one of my mother's caretakers, was talking with her and asked, "How did you raise your six girls? Tell me what you did so I can do the same with my children." Ma replied, "I didn't do anything. But no one will ever know how much I prayed." Adeline asked her if she was eager to see her husband again. Ma answered, "Yes. But I want to see my Savior first of all."

17

Chief

Mupati uwuminwa aalimuzimbwa.
A respected person is beaten when you are trying to kill a tsetse fly on them.

A heavy rain in the a.m. 7:30–11:00. Typing programme for graduation, etc. Not feeling well. Feverish, diarrhea, headache. Home from 11:00–13:00. District Governor called that he is coming, also Chief Macha and one Headman. Making final preparations.

January 25, 1985

Malaria was a regular visitor in Arlene's life in Africa, especially in Macha. If she was feeling ill, her first thought was to consider a blood smear to test for malaria. During the rainy season, Macha was one of the world's malaria hot spots and therefore a valuable candidate for malaria research. Enter Dr. Phil Thuma.

When Arlene arrived at Macha, Phil was the chief pediatrician on staff at Macha Mission Hospital. He was also Arlene's colleague and took regular responsibilities in lecturing at the school. Phil's father was Alvan Thuma, a legendary doctor in that region of the world. In 1951, when Phil was a babe in arms, Alvan and his wife, Ardys, moved to Africa. In essence, Phil was a native of Central Africa. He learned English and *Chitonga* (the language of the Tonga people) side by side. He watched the Macha Mission Hospital go up brick by brick, probably even carrying a few bricks to his daddy, who often took his turn beside the bricklayers.

Phil returned to the States to receive his medical training at Templeton, but his heart never left Africa. After returning to Macha, he specifically felt God calling him to care for the children of Central Africa. He responded to that call by returning to the States to do pediatric training at Johns Hopkins. Arlene saw in Phil a disciplined worker, a superb organizer, and an astute student of culture. Both of them had been around tribal community enough to know that one must respect their politics. When Phil set out to work on the malaria problem of the Macha catchment, he proved to be an exemplary politician.

There was a buzzing sound. A young man wearing cardboard wings and a mask with an absurdly long, narrow proboscis darted and hovered here and there among the audience, attempting to poke people who dodged out of the way. Chief Macha, in on the joke, sat on the platform, still and unafraid. Finally, the largest mosquito in the world fixed its gaze on the chief and let out a shout. A drum beat supported the escalating danger. The huge insect bobbed and weaved more narrowly now as it slowly flew closer and closer to the chief. The crowd called out, "Nooooo!" and "Watch out!" and "Kill it!" Arriving in position behind the chief, the mosquito raised its stinger high into the air and lowered it toward the chief's shoulder, as the drummer built the cadence to a crescendo. When the stinger touched the chief, the percussionist ended with a tremendous whack, and in the pursuing space of silence, the actor playing the insect made a great sucking sound. Pulling its stinger off the chief's arm, the insect let out a satisfied "Ahhhhhh!" and flew straight away. The crowd booed but could not help beaming with delight at the skit.

"The mosquito bit the chief!" someone shouted. "The mosquito bit Chief Macha!"

"Have some respect, mosquito!"

Someone repeated the title of the most respected man in the region, and it immediately became a chant. "Chief Macha! Chief Macha! Chief Macha!"

The chief rose to his feet, and the entire audience also rose, applauding. He raised his hand, and they grew quiet. He gestured for them to sit, and they did. The chief then spoke. "The mosquitos do not know who the chief is. But the chief knows who the doctor is. And I would like Dr. Thuma to say what he wants to say."

Phil stood as the chief gave him the floor.

"*Twalumba* [Thank you], Chief Macha. As many of you know, I was brought here as a child, a baby from the United States. I learned to speak from *Batonga* [the Tonga people]. You knew my father, Dr. Alvan. God has given me a desire to bring healing everywhere, but especially to Africa. God has put the people of Africa in my heart, especially Africa's children. I have heard *Batonga* wailing for your children while I work at the Macha Hospital. I cannot ignore this sound. *Batonga* are wailing because the children are dying. So many children die of malaria. This disease is a friend of the mosquito. And we have many mosquitos in Macha. I stand here today to ask Chief Macha to give me permission to find out what the mosquito does when it bites. I will need the chief's help. And I will need the help of many people. I wait for the chief's answer."

Chief Macha stepped forward and held out his hand. Phil took the chief's hand, while at the same time grabbing his own forearm and bending a knee in respect. The audience applauded. Everyone knew that a significant venture had begun, but no one could have predicted the good it would bring.

During the 1980s, as Dr. Phil had noted, the soundtrack of Macha mission life included wailing. "Someone died," the wailer cried, and if the dead person was a child, a probable cause was malaria. By the mid-1980s, the hospital was admitting nearly a thousand malaria patients per year to its pediatric wards. Most survived, but not all. Those who worked at the mission tried to ignore this wailing, pushing it into the background, so they could get on with their tasks. Phil, however, would never allow himself to stop hearing it. That sound reminded him of his calling. He had profound respect for malaria but was determined to beat it back.

A personal motivation for him was the witness of Marie Ann Traver, who had been only about four years younger than Phil. Marie grew up in the Brethren in Christ Church near the rural community of Wainfleet, Ontario, not far from Niagara Falls. After studying at Messiah College in Pennsylvania, at age twenty-two she was called to a three-year term at the Macha hospital and school. Phil knew Marie only by reputation, because malaria took her before he returned from his own medical studies.

Marie's encounter with malaria was sudden, a matter of days: bites, fever, blood test, medication, jaundice, hospitalization, coma, and last breath. After her death, this prayer was found in her journal, dated April 17, written three months into her time at Macha.

> My years at Macha are well on their way
> > going by a little too quickly—
> The sand of time seems to be becoming
> > finer and finer.
>
> Anxiety comes
> > when I imagine what emptiness my years here could bring.
> Emptiness—not for me, but for those whom I've been sent to.
> Lord forbid—three years of pleasures, lovely letters home,
> > albums of striking photographs.
> Many meals of roast beef and apple pie and strawberry jam,
> > hours of sewing attractive Java prints and African patterns.
>
> Three years of Crystapen injections and correcting students
> > on how they taped the Darrow's bottle.

Three years of feeding the dog and cat and making
    cookies for prayer meeting.
Three years of keeping a balance
    between sending tapes and receiving them.
Three years of "vanity"—Lord forbid it.

I am asking you to take me these fleeting years
To pour me out when and where you choose.
To help me give of myself unreservedly,
    first to you, and then through you to others.
May my growing love for Jesus be evident in me.
Help me to sow your seed, or else to water some another has sown.

May I encourage instead of criticize.
Love instead of shun.
And now that I have given these years to you
I trust the outcome also, to you.

Lord, I do not ask to become well-known or "famous,"
    for lack of a better word.
Those who have known me may forget,
    as long as they remember you.
Forgive for the times I've built a lovely image of myself
    I'd like others to see.
I am not so holy, I am the least and yet
    am what I am because of Jesus.
I do not know what I may become . . .
I may return home to serve in my parents' house
And once again be a daughter and a sister and aunt
    to those I love but left.
You may choose to bring me here again
    or to another land, though that I doubt.
And, Lord, I can't forget
    that you may even come, and take me home.

Marie was one of many missionaries to fight malaria. Arlene lost track of the number of times she had contracted malaria while living on the African continent. She first faced it in the Sudan. There was no vaccine, but there were medications to mitigate the symptoms and attack the parasites once a mosquito deposited them in the blood stream. The symptoms were varied, mimicking many other illnesses. Arlene often ached in every muscle, her head pounded, her fever rose, and the flu-like symptoms of nausea and diarrhea often joined the fray.

She got a respite while living in the mountains of Ethiopia where the high altitudes were not friendly to the breeding of mosquitos. The danger resumed when she moved to Katete, but it was worst of all at Macha.

As soon as Arlene's colleagues tested positive, some would take a brief holiday to get as far away as they could from mosquitos and work, taking the necessary time to rest and recuperate. Who could blame them? However, Arlene never felt as if her position afforded the luxury of a pause. She forced herself to go on.

The recommended medications kept changing. In the Sudan, she sometimes took quinine, but that medication made her feel sick for a full week. In general, the drugs she used in the 1960s at Nasir seemed to have little effect on 1980s Macha malaria: the parasite had mutated. Phil often prescribed Fansidar (sulfadoxine/pyrimethamine) sometimes combining it with a two-week course of tetracycline or a mixture including proguanil. Arlene became concerned about a side effect called agranulocytosis, which results in low white blood cell count, putting her at risk for additional illnesses, chronic infections, sores, dizziness, and general lack of energy. She often had sleeplessness, or when she did sleep, she had vivid nightmares. Undergoing malaria treatment sometimes made it unsafe to drive. Once she tried mefloquine, and it was the closest she ever came to being drunk. Under its influence, she could hardly even stand. Given her responsibilities with the General Nursing Council, she would sometimes forgo any medication and drive to the capital, illness and all. Arlene was not certain it mattered all that much anyway, since the cure often felt worse than the sickness.

One day, Phil Thuma would demonstrate to Chief Macha and the entire scientific world that malaria could be brought to its knees—but unfortunately not until after Arlene had left Zambia. That feat would take financial resources, creative thought, community support, discipline, faith, and time.

For now, malaria was winning. During her final year in Macha, Arlene contracted malaria ten times in a single rainy season.

18

Doris

Kuzyala kwachembele nkumwi.
Somebody's child is also your child.

---

*To school at 5:45 p.m. All of the Nurses Training School
staff were there for the announcement for Set 28. They
reacted in shock and disbelief that all had passed!
Typed invitation for graduation. Doris typed all day on
letters in response to new applicants.*

January 23, 1985

Arlene had an excellent office manager in Mrs. Chizonde, and
she was crucial to the operation of the school. In the days before
the ubiquity of personal computers, near-perfect typing skills were
extremely valuable—and Mrs. Chizonde was certainly skilled in
that area. With her help, Arlene's disciplined leadership and exact-
ing standards transformed the Zambia Enrolled Nursing School at
Macha into one of the best in the country.

Every six months, over a thousand applications arrived from
around the country. Zambia-trained nurses were in high demand,
not only in their home country but also in Europe. The file of
each applicant required meticulous attention as that prospective
nurse moved through the process of application, culling, written
testing, interviews, acceptance and matriculation, examinations,
and graduation. In addition, the office manager shepherded staff
communications, mimeographing, supply ordering, and assisting
in the scheduling of nurse-training rotations at the hospital. Mrs.

Chizonde had a big job, and she was good at it. But she set her sights on other opportunities, and shortly after Christmas 1984, the community celebrated her service at a farewell party. Although Mrs. Chizonde seemed irreplaceable, Arlene set about trying.

During Mrs. Chizonde's final days, while Arlene interviewed potential replacements, a local young woman named Doris stepped in to help. Doris had been working on the cleaning staff at the school. When Mrs. Chizonde was gone and a replacement had not yet been secured, Arlene asked Doris to take over the office work for a day. When she did well, Arlene offered her the job.

Doris held the position for the remainder of Arlene's years at Macha. She had a joyful servant's heart and a professional attitude. She lived near the mission and had fine language skills in both Tonga and English. When the faculty had its tensions, as all faculties do, she kept her head down and quietly focused on her tasks. Years later, Arlene would remember her as "my good, good secretary, someone who helped me so much."

Things were looking good from Doris's point of view also. She had landed a stable job with a fine supervisor near her home. What she did not know was that a deadly disease, birthed decades earlier northwest of Zambia, was heading toward her.

In the 1920s in Kinshasa, the overpopulated capital city of the Democratic Republic of Congo, a virus flowed from a chimpanzee to a human. It was not an airborne virus, but one that was carried in the blood or other bodily fluid. The virus-that-did-not-yet-have-a-name was years in its incubation phase, a phase without symptoms. By the time the virus became symptomatic within its host, it was likely to have already infected others.

The spread of the virus was assisted by the new highway system out of Kinshasa. The great road extended to the east and veered southward into the Copperbelt, eventually following the Line of

Rail that traveled down through Kitwe, Lusaka, Choma, Livingston, and on to South Africa. Roads and trains brought strangers together, and some of those strangers had sexual encounters, so the virus-that-did-not-yet-have-a-name quietly killed its hosts and went undetected for decades.

To keep up on the world, Arlene subscribed to *TIME* magazine. Its September 6, 1982, issue included the first full-page article describing a medical condition that seemed to be an American or perhaps Haitian illness connected to a particular segment of society. The illness had been assigned a name: acquired immunodeficiency syndrome—or AIDS. The first paragraph of the article read as follows:

> It began suddenly in the autumn of 1979. Young homosexual men with a history of promiscuity started showing up at the medical clinics of New York City, Los Angeles, and San Francisco with a bizarre array of ailments.

The syndrome was not yet fully connected to the virus that traced back to Kinshasa and would eventually be named Human Immunodeficiency Virus or HIV. Since HIV in the United States revealed its impact primarily in the gay community, it became known by many as GRID (Gay-Related Immune Deficiency), "gay cancer," or "gay plague."

On October 15, 1982, at a White House press conference, reporter Lester Kinsolving asked Larry Speakes, President Reagan's deputy press secretary, about AIDS. The following is transcribed from a recording of that interview:

> KINSOLVING: Larry, does the president have any reaction to the announcement by the Center for Disease Control in Atlanta that A.I.D.S. is now an epidemic in 600, over 600 cases?
>
> SPEAKES: A.I.D.S.? I haven't got anything on it.

KINSOLVING: And over a third of them have died. It's known as "gay plague." *(Laughter erupted from the pool of reporters.)* No. It is. I mean it's a pretty serious thing that, uh, one in every three people that get this have died. And I wonder if the president is aware of this.

SPEAKES: I don't have it. Are you . . . do you?

KINSOLVING: You don't have it? Well, I'm relieved to hear that, Larry. *(More laughter was heard in the room.)* I'm delighted.

SPEAKES: You didn't answer my question.

KINSOLVING: No, I don't.

SPEAKES: How do you know?

KINSOLVING: Does the president . . . in other words, the White House looks on this as a great joke?

SPEAKES: No, I don't know anything about it, Lester.

By the time of that press conference, Arlene was back in Macha following her short visit to the States due to her mother's death. Although Arlene didn't witness that press conference, she did have a similar experience at one of her General Nursing Council meetings. In a conversation about the cause of HIV/AIDS, she mentioned studies that indicated it was spread through sex. The room broke into laughter. Arlene was shocked that medical professionals couldn't speak of the exchange of bodily fluids without giggling like junior high students.

To make the challenge worse, some leaders in the American Christian community labeled HIV/AIDS as "God's curse on homosexual behavior." That pronouncement made it easier for these Christians to turn aside from assisting those infected, believing "they brought it on themselves" and asking, "Who am I to stand between God and his intended curse?" Arlene, on the other hand, never felt for a moment that she should stand back from providing medical care, no matter who may have been at "fault" regarding an illness, disease, syndrome, or injury.

There was, of course, a difference between fault-finding and identifying the cause of an illness, so that the transmission might be avoided in the future. Sexual activity with more than one person did seem to multiply the risk. In the case of Zambian demographics, there was no certainty as to an individual's promiscuity, but there was evidence that on average young males might have as many as ten different partners in a single month.

The date of HIV's arrival in Macha is uncertain. It's possible it was already incubating in Doris's body when she started her job at the Nurses Training School, even though there was no indication of it yet. In her second full year in the office, she went on vacation. When she returned, Arlene was deeply grateful and wrote in her journal,

> *Doris is back from holiday today. A big relief to have her help now again. She got Set 35 acceptance packets ready to mail. Started on 77 refusal letters.*

In what seemed to be an unrelated entry, Arlene wrote in her journal a week later that she saw a man on a motorcycle ride by with a coffin strapped onto the seat behind him. More remarkable than the image of a coffin on a motorcycle was the fact that Arlene described it as "a common picture here."

The commonality of death in the African bush may have contributed to the difficulty in fighting the disease. Zambians mourned every death, but they expected it and weren't afraid. Although they might fear the dying journey, they were not likely to change their behavior due to the threat of death itself.

By the end of 1986, HIV had finally reared its ugly head in Macha. That year, the Macha Mission Hospital cared for nine AIDS patients. At that point, Doris was still healthy and productive. She was fine.

While many in the American church still assumed that AIDS was a gay disease, the medical staff at Macha had a much wider understanding. African AIDS was a rising pandemic that especially impacted sexually active young adults—and their children. Arlene unflinchingly shared Macha's AIDS statistics with her home church, and Phil Thuma presented a paper on the disease to the General Conference of the Brethren in Christ Church.

At the end of 1987, when the statistics were tallied, 150 AIDS patients had been cared for at Macha that year. Thirty of those patients died at the hospital, while many others went home to die.

The task of education then began. Arlene explained to her students that AIDS was not spread by mosquitos and could not be picked up by using a public toilet. Speaking quite openly, Arlene encouraged her students to avoid sex before marriage and, if they got married, both husband and wife should limit sex to one's spouse. Even as she made these suggestions, she knew this was a polygamous culture and that sexual boundaries were understood to be different for men and women. There were, therefore, many reasons for the students' eyes to glaze over when Arlene spoke of human sexuality and AIDS. Arlene's final commendation was to encourage her students to at least use a condom since that might afford some protection.

Some of the information about AIDS began to sink in, but not precisely in the way Arlene had hoped. Her student nurses began to flinch at the thought of caring for the growing number of AIDS patients. Some were not convinced that the disease could spread from person to person, while others wondered whether the virus could be airborne and spread like the flu. If so, it might be dangerous to be in its presence. Some student nurses therefore refused to touch AIDS patients, asking for different assignments on the hospital schedule.

Arlene attempted to balance both freedom and responsibility. The administration agreed they wouldn't require nurses, whether students or staff, to fulfill a task they felt put them in personal danger. At the same time, nurses were urged to base their decisions on science rather than fear.

On Monday, November 23, 1987, the temperature in Macha peaked over 100 degrees, while the rainy season was trying to begin, sputtering out some drops for a few days. Each morning at 6:00 a.m. when it was still cool, Doris came to the office to work. She took three hours off at midday and then worked again in the late afternoon, saying goodbye at 5:00 p.m.

That Monday, Arlene found a note from Doris, asking for the following Monday off because she planned to get married on the weekend. Arlene was stunned—the whole thing was sudden and secretive. She wondered if Doris was too afraid to ask in person, because the request came at the most inopportune time—when the external examiners would be in town to evaluate the practical nursing skills of Set 34.

Later that week, Doris changed her mind about her wedding date and invited Arlene to attend her wedding on the first Sunday in December. Arlene welcomed the invitation and found her way to the village of the family's medicine man where a crowd had gathered. Along with others, Arlene waited for three hours. Food was set out and consumed, but still the bride did not arrive. Since it would be dark soon, Arlene went home without seeing Doris in her wedding dress, let alone being able to witness her wedding.

The truth eventually came partially to light. At the time of the wedding, Doris was five months pregnant and her husband was terribly ill. A few months later, when Doris went on maternity leave, her husband entered the hospital with, as far as Arlene understood, tuberculosis and AIDS. Arlene went to visit them at their home when the baby was a few months old. Although Doris's husband seemed stronger at that time, he soon went downhill.

Doris returned to work and remained the office manager during the transition to Arlene's replacement when Arlene retired. Arlene never learned what happened to Doris's husband or baby; but after she was back in Sioux Center, she received word that Doris had died of AIDS, which suggested she may have been HIV positive the entire time she worked with Arlene. So much, though, was rumor, innuendo, and speculation. Arlene never did find out anything for certain. Such was the nature of a disease surrounded by shame and recrimination, rather than the usual empathy and healing care that every nurse is taught to provide. In 1988, the AIDS patient count at Macha grew to over three hundred. It would, of course, get much, much worse.

19

Angels

Uuyenda nguubimba.
One traveling must tremble.

---

*Woke up at 4 a.m. with headache. "You shall live
a long good life, like standing grain, you'll not be
harvested until it's time" (Job 5:26). Went to church
and it being the first Sunday of the year, it was a time
of testimony . . . very nice. Decided to sit outside under
the tree. Set 35 came to sing "Happy Birthday."*

January 3, 1988

One

In mid-January 1988, Arlene was in Lusaka for General Nursing
Council meetings. On the last Sunday of the month, she arose in
the predawn dark to load the car in preparation for her five-hour
return drive to Macha. By sunrise, she was ready to roll out of the
city. She inserted a worship cassette into her tape player and drove
southward out of the city. As morning gilded the skies, her heart
awakening cried, "May Jesus Christ be praised!"

In an hour or so, her 1981 white Datsun Stanza sedan began
its descent into the gorge of the Kafue River. When her 1971 blue
Datsun had begun nickel-and-diming her toward poverty with its
constant repairs, Arlene flew to South Africa to purchase a newer
used car from a missionary-network contact who managed a large

car dealership southwest of Johannesburg. The Stanza had served her well for the past three years.

After crossing the Kafue Bridge, Arlene pressed the gas to support the climb up the escarpment. At the brow of the hill, she suddenly came upon a broken-down tractor trailer under repair directly in front of her on the road. To make matters worse, three long-horned black cows were attempting to cross the road between Arlene and the truck. When their handlers saw Arlene's car, they leapt in front of the cows to drive them back. She knew she was about to hit the cows or the men or the truck or veer off into the bush. Before anything happened, however, she stopped the car, amazed that she didn't hit anything or anyone or get stuck on the side of the road. It seemed miraculous. While she sat frozen, catching her breath, she watched as the cattle and men safely crossed over. She finally inched past the broken truck and continued on her way.

This near-accident was common on Zambian highway as vehicles seldom pulled off to the side if they had engine troubles. The road itself was typically the only paved surface on these highways. The shoulder, if there was one at all, was dirt or mud. To pull off the road was to risk never being able to return without help from a tow. Consequently, what was once a two-lane road might suddenly become one lane.

Africa is a pathway continent. Most paths are narrow and used for walking, biking, or herding animals. Some of these paths eventually become paved roads. While paved roads have obvious advantages for traveling, pavement creates dangers, especially if pedestrians continue to use the same route of travel. In Arlene's time, African highways were not well-policed, and pedestrians—who often walked on the highways with their animals—didn't perceive that vehicles had the right of way. Pedestrians, animals, and trucks broken down in the middle of the road were regular challenges for all drivers, including Arlene.

Despite her surprising encounter that morning, Arlene made it safely to Macha just before noon—hot, weary, and thankful to

God for a safe arrival. She wrote in her journal that night that an Invisible Hand had slowed her car to a full stop at the brow of the hill on the Kafue escarpment.

Two

In her role as chair of the Disciplinary Committee of the General Nursing Council, Arlene had to attend a series of meetings in the capital. On Wednesday, April 27, 1988, she was up early and had enough time to make a pancake breakfast for herself. She taught a class, finished some correspondence, and was driving off mission property by 8:40 a.m. She decided to take the Choma Road so she could stop at the bank and also pick up a couple of passengers.

In 1988, the Choma Road was not one of those that were paved. The rainy season was pretty much over, which meant two things. First, grass that had been growing during the rainy season remained uncut, crowded up to the road, and was taller than Arlene's car. Second, once the road dried out from all the rain, grading equipment smoothed out the ruts that had developed during the season. Arlene thought the road must have been graded fairly recently because it seemed smoother than ever before. This enabled her to travel 45 miles per hour without any of the usual bone-jarring vibrations.

When the road was eventually paved, the more dangerous curves were lengthened to make them safer. But on this particular Wednesday, Arlene entered one of those sharp curves with tall grass on either side, a few miles north of the turnoff to the game farm. Once she was deep in this curving tunnel of grass, she saw a blue truck coming right at her—going too fast and taking up her side of the road. She instinctively shouted "God, help!" as she braked and yanked the steering wheel to the side, taking her chances with whatever danger the unknown tall grass was hiding rather than plow straight into the huge, flat-faced truck. The front fender of her car managed to miss the truck's bumper, but she heard a sharp pop as the other vehicle barreled past her. Her car kept going, but it was all grass—there was no tree, no boulder, no ravine. Her car continued in its arc, coming to a stop facing the truck as it sped away.

Arlene turned off the ignition and stepped out—thanking and praising God she was still alive. Looking around the car, she discovered what must have made the popping sound: her side mirror was smashed. She tried to walk, but her legs grew wobbly. Needing to sit down, she climbed back into the driver's seat, even though she wasn't ready to drive back through the grass to the roadway. She looked down at her dashboard and stared at the sliver of paper some previous owner had taped there:

When she finally calmed, she got out of the car and walked through the tall grass to ensure there was a clear path back to the road. Returning to the car, she drove through the grass to the roadway, checking carefully that no one was coming. She then drove through the curve, praying and singing. The song that first sprang to her mind was one she had heard a woman named Estelle sing at her home church, which was a contemporary song when Arlene was young.

> I sing because I'm happy.
> I sing because I'm free;
> For his eye is on the sparrow,
> And I know he watches me.

She wondered if someone in Sioux Center woke up between 1:00 and 2:00 that Wednesday morning with an impulse to pray for her. She never knew, but she still wondered.

Two days later, on her return trip to Macha, she pulled over in the center of the curve and saw her tracks in the grass. She got out and stood there again because that spot had become Holy Ground. Later that year, at the time of her retirement, Arlene sold the white Stanza. But before she handed over the keys, she peeled the verse from Psalm 91 off the dash and transferred it to her journal as a remembrance of what had happened that day.

Three

On Sunday, August 7, 1988, Arlene woke at 4:45 a.m. to drive her friend Rhonda, a short-term missionary, to the airport in Lusaka. Knowing that Rhonda might not make this trip again and that even Arlene's time in Zambia was winding down, they stopped a few times along the way to greet friends and check if anyone else needed a ride to the capital city that morning. A man named Abraham accepted the offer.

The trip went smoothly. They descended into the Kafue River gorge from the southwest, crossed the bridge, and began the climb toward the town of Kafue—stuck behind a huge army truck laboring slowly up the hill. Since Arlene could clearly see that no one was coming, she pulled into the passing lane. As she came alongside the truck, moving into his blind spot, the driver of the truck veered into her, denting the side of her car and cracking her windshield.

No one was hurt, but since they were near a town, the police needed to be brought to the scene. The army truck stopped and eight men got out to wait with her and the others for the police. The Kafue police had no vehicle and took an hour getting to the accident site. Although the driver of the army truck had neither braked nor signaled, the police found Arlene at fault since there was a crossroad present that made her attempt to pass illegal.

Abraham decided to go his own way at Kafue, and Arlene and Rhonda limped into Lusaka a few hours late. They made it to the evening worship service at the International Church. After the service, Rhonda made a phone call home to Michigan and learned that her cousin had been killed in a car accident.

Regarding her encounter that day with the army, Arlene wrote in her journal,

I remained very calm and experienced peace. It could have been so serious.

She had to pay a 50 kwacha fine for careless driving. There was no damage to the army truck, but Arlene had to leave her car for several weeks at Panelbeaters, an auto repair shop in Choma.

When the shop couldn't find a replacement windshield anywhere in Zambia, they managed to find a new one in South Africa. Someone from the Southern Baptist mission brought it up to Choma on one of their supply runs.

Four

Monday, September 12, 1988, was an extremely busy day. Awake at 4:15 a.m., Arlene was at the school an hour later. The day was filled with lectures and the usual array of administrative meetings. At 7:00 p.m., some visitors arrived from Choma, bringing the good news that her car would be ready to be picked up the next day from Panelbeaters.

When Arlene locked the office door after 8:00 p.m., she used her flashlight on her walk home. About five steps from her front door, she felt something cold and damp brush her leg. Glancing down, she saw a huge cobra, coiled and raised, ready to strike. She backed into the house to grab a weapon—not wanting to let it get away, because one encounter with it was enough.

Moments later, she returned with ax in hand. Although the snake hadn't moved, Arlene was rethinking her plan. It was clearly too dark to be fighting a snake alone. She called out for help, but the only person who came was a little neighbor girl, who picked up a small stick and flung it at the snake. The cobra merely lowered itself and slithered away. A few days later, the neighbors reported spotting a cobra in their yard, but they had not been quick enough to kill it.

Five

The next day, Arlene picked up her white Stanza from Panelbeaters. On the way home, the trunk popped open. After trying to close it, she snapped off a vine from the roadside and used it to tie the trunk shut until she could get the lock welded. Some odd vibrations remained, but the car functioned well enough to move her from one place to another. Arlene's schedule did not afford her the opportunity to be picky.

Later in the same week as the cobra incident, Arlene again crossed her yard in the dark, this time early in the morning. She had General Nursing Council meetings in Lusaka and decided to leave by 4:00 a.m., even though that meant driving before sunrise.

Wide awake, she said her morning prayers as she drove. As she passed the place where the truck had forced her off into the high grass, her mind wandered back to that day—and then before she knew it, she was at Fisher's Bridge and had to slam on her brakes! This dangerous, one-lane bridge tended to catch her off guard, even when she knew it was coming. It was startling enough in the daytime, but coming across it in the dark was really frightening.

Although there were no signs warning vehicles to slow down before proceeding, a slow crossing was wise. This narrow bridge, which was located around a sharp curve and down a dip in the road, had no protective guardrails and had been the scene of several accidents. Ironically, it was named "Fisher's Bridge" after a missionary who drove a truck off it on his first trip from Macha to Choma. Arlene's other recent brushes with danger didn't help her already-frayed nerves on this particular Thursday morning.

As she crept her way across Fisher's Bridge, threading the needle through the low concrete bumpers that pretended to be guardrails, she realized that moments before she had been praying, asking God for an assurance of his love. On the other side of the bridge, she burst into an intense prayer in tongues. Subsequently, something unusual happened: Arlene received the interpretation of the prayer. That night she wrote in her journal what she could remember of the interpretation:

My child, My child, My child, I do care for you. I do protect you. I love you very much. Be assured of My love. I know all your

weaknesses but do not be discouraged. I love you in spite of your
weaknesses and failures. I love you just as you are, for you are
my child.

She would later say of that incident, "God spoke to me and healed
me there."

On January 3, 1989, Arlene turned sixty-five. Later that month,
she retired from her assignment as head tutor of Macha Mission's
nursing school along with her various assignments with Zambia's
General Nursing Council. On Arlene's final Sunday at Macha, the
rainy season was underway.

Waking with a headache, she wondered if she had contracted
malaria again. She lay praying underneath her protective mosquito
netting. Although it wasn't raining, it was steamy and hot that morning when she walked to church and took her seat on the women's
side. She knew that Pastor Mudenda would call her forward to say
some farewell words. She had written what she planned to say on
a small, blue card.

Thank you for allowing me to be a guest in your country. I never
intended to stay forever, and the time has come for me to leave.
I know that God led me here. I have assurance that this is His
time for me to go.

Thank you for accepting me as I am . . . with my many faults
and weaknesses. I'm sorry if my frank, straightforward manner
may have offended you. I'm sorry that I did not learn Tonga. I
just could not seem to find the time or energy to do everything
I wanted to do.

I'm grateful that God has provided persons who are more capable
than I to take over where I leave off.

At that point in her short speech, she planned to mention some specific names.

At the appropriate moment, the pastor did call on Arlene, and she walked to the platform. She spoke in English, and a man named Jonah stood beside her to translate into Tonga. Arlene took one look at the congregation and said, "With a heart of thanksgiving—" but then started weeping. The church grew dead quiet. She tried to speak through tears, but her sobbing was the only intelligible language. Finally, she shook her head at Jonah. As she stepped off the platform, someone began to sing, and the whole room joined in:

> Blest be the tie that binds
> Our hearts in Christian love.
> The fellowship of kindred minds
> Is like to that above.

20

Chapel

Chito nchuzibide chilumya ntale.
A river crossing that you are used to can still
bring a crocodile bite.

---

*Up at 4 a.m. and left at 5 a.m. with David Pollock by
taxi to Coimbatore. Very dark as we rode the curvy
hillside. Fire along road at one place. Scary. But very
interesting to visit with David Pollock who became a
Christian as a result of the death of five missionaries
to the Aucas. Good flight from Coimbatore to Bombay.
Centaur Hotel overnight. Repacking to prepare for
colder weather and overseas flight. Thank you. Thank
you, dear God. It has been such a good trip so far.*

February 28, 1989

Arlene's homecoming was full of gladness, in part because she
retained her birth culture's tendency to hide heartbreak, even from
oneself. She appeared calm as she handed her passport to the federal
agent at Kennedy International Airport in Queens, New York. She
had done this ritual so many times before, but this pass through
customs could be her last.

After decades of living in east Africa, Arlene was moving permanently to where she was born, a little town tucked away in the
northwest corner of Iowa. She would now see white faces almost
exclusively. She was migrating from a place where her white face
was the anomaly among very dark-skinned people. She sometimes

forgot that she herself was Caucasian. Perhaps it was her sudden awareness of her own whiteness that caused her to take special note of the custom officer's black skin. She felt a sudden stab of sorrow, but did what she usually did in such circumstances: she smiled.

"What was the reason for your trip overseas, ma'am?"

"I've been a missionary nurse in Africa for thirty-four years. I'm coming home to retire." He stamped her passport and said, "Well done. And welcome home."

Arlene marked his response. Later that night, the first of March, she wrote his words in her journal. She would examine and re-examine those words. "Well done. And welcome home."

Done.

Home.

It had been forty-nine days since Arlene departed Macha, Zambia, and her one-story condo built with bricks made of termite dung. Starting on January 11, she had journeyed through Choma, Lusaka, Nairobi, Addis Ababa, Jimma, Mettu, Gore, Bombay, Coimbatore, Kodai Kanal, and now New York City and North Brunswick, visiting with friends and debriefing with mission officials. On Saturday, a snowstorm stalled her connecting flight in Chicago. But on Sunday afternoon, she finally stepped off the plane in Sioux Falls and walked into the arms of three of her five sisters and their extended families. An hour's ride through the snow-covered fields carried her across the South Dakota border into Iowa and toward her hometown of Sioux Center.

Grada drove while Arlene busily surveyed the scene outside the car for any changes since she had last been home. Sister Bernice and her husband, Howard, rode in the back seat. They were now traveling on what was once known as the KT (the King of Trails). This once grand highway was devised to carry traffic from Winnipeg to Galveston, slicing mid-America in half from north to south. The national interstate system surpassed the KT by the time of Arlene's homecoming in 1989, and now KT's traffic was regional at best. The KT was now known simply as Highway 75, and the Sioux County towns had become islands unto themselves.

One of the harbingers of home was the white steeple of the diminutive Wayside Chapel, nestled among the trees along Highway 75 just north of Sioux Center. The ten-foot by fourteen-foot sanctuary had barely enough room for twelve disciples to crowd in for prayer.

Across the road from the chapel, the Broek farm had a Bible verse painted on a sheet of plywood fixed upright to the peak of their barn roof. It was not the actual words, just the reference: *Phil 2:3*. If you didn't know your Bible, you might think that the barn sign was advertising a hybrid of seed corn. But this was northwest Iowa, and most residents were faithful church attenders and knew their Bible. So, most people cruising by the Broek farm knew they were seeing a reminder to be a good neighbor, or at least they knew where to look up the verse when they got home.

Do nothing out of selfish ambition or vain conceit. Rather, in humility value others above yourselves. (Philippians 2:3)

Just after the chapel, Grada turned the car west at County Road B30, moving onto gravel and then over railroad tracks. As soon as they crossed the tracks, Arlene could see the family farm—the place Grandpa Schuiteman had homesteaded in 1897. He eventually tendered the farm to Arlene's Ma and Pa, who would then pass it down to their girls. Bernice and Howard lived there now.

The cozy two-story farmhouse was the same as it was when Arlene and her sisters were born there. South of the house were a silo, hog house, cow barn, horse barn, chicken coop, and corncrib. To the north was the grove where Ma, the family's lover of trees, planted silver-tipped Russian olives neatly in a row to slow down the winds that plowed in from the northwest. Two more tidy rows, one of ash and one of apple, finished out the grove. Ma used to have Arlene and her sisters rake the grove twice a year, spring and fall. Raking days were glory days, resulting in leaf piles and bonfires. Every spring, when Ma caught her first glimpse of buds in the grove, she had a ritual of speaking aloud the Alfred Joyce Kilmer 1914 poem she had learned as a young woman:

I think that I shall never see
A poem lovely as a tree.

A tree whose hungry mouth is prest
Against the earth's sweet flowing breast;

A tree that looks at God all day,
And lifts her leafy arms to pray;

A tree that may in Summer wear
A nest of robins in her hair;

Upon whose bosom snow has lain;
Who intimately lives with rain.

Poems are made by fools like me,
But only God can make a tree.

It was not spring now, but one glimpse of the grove, and Arlene could almost hear Ma saying, "I think that I shall never see . . ."

Bernice invited Arlene and Grada in for a snack, but the invitation was mostly out of politeness. The kindest thing was to get Arlene to town and allow her to rest after her arduous journey across multiple continents.

Bernice and Howard said good night and waved as Grada navigated the car out of the frozen farmyard. Coming past Kroon's corner on the north side of Sioux Center, Arlene saw the glow of her little town. She had returned here off and on over her thirty-four years as an African, watching the signs on the storefronts change. Now as dusk slipped into dark, Arlene's memories returned to the stores of her childhood: De Kraay's Drug (and soda fountain), Te Paske Law, DeRuyter Hardware, Roelofs Groceries, De Bruin Shoes, Ida Mulder Beauty Shop, Schalekamp's Drug Store, De Jong Hatchery, and Mouw Motor.

The car passed the Farmer's Co-op where Grada served as the accountant, calculating seedtime and harvest for much of the surrounding countryside. Over the years of Arlene's absences, her hometown had transitioned from a village into a city, five thousand strong. The Dutch stores had mostly disappeared into modern franchises: Casey's, Hardees, and—way off in the strip mall on the southside—Walmart. They came to the hospital where their parents had each departed this world. Grada turned east. A few more blocks, and they were turning into the driveway of their home.

Some ladies from the church had taped a heart-shaped welcome-home sign to the door. This was the modest one-story house Pa and Ma built shortly after Arlene left for Africa the first time. As Arlene entered the house, she felt the familiar stab that Pa's heart attack had come too soon after their move to town. Arlene wished she could hear his whistle as she moved from the throughway into the kitchen. Pa would have filled the house with joy on her final return from the mission field. He would have been entertaining all of them while Ma, the consummate cook, filled the air with aromas to welcome Arlene home. There would have been chicken, boiled potatoes and gravy, corn, Jell-O salad, apple pie, and warm bread, timed to come out of the oven when their daughters arrived, just like when the six girls consumed an entire loaf immediately after school on Fridays, Ma's weekly bread-baking day. Arlene paused in the middle of the kitchen, listening to the silence.

Grada—a quiet, no-nonsense person—nudged past Arlene to haul in the first round of luggage into Ma's old bedroom. The Schuiteman girls had inherited the house, and it was now Grada's residence and also Arlene's when she was on furlough. She would now live here permanently.

Permanently.

After emptying the car, they examined the beautifully decorated cake gracing the kitchen counter where Ma's pie would have been cooling. The cake, like the sign, was from the "Rebecca Circle," a group of Arlene's prayer and financial supporters. Arlene's whole church was eager to welcome her and expected her at the morning service before her itinerary got disrupted.

Word would now be traveling around town that Arlene had arrived safely, in spite of the snowstorm. She decided she was not up to attending the evening service—she would listen to it on the radio. But before the pastor even read the Scripture passage, she had fallen asleep.

Arlene woke at 2:30 a.m., jet-lagged and unsure of where she was. She remembered walking up a gangplank at the age of thirty-one. Now she was back out of Africa, lying in a bed in Iowa at sixty-five.

Those years flashed by, and her vocation as a missionary nurse was gone. She suddenly felt sad, so desperately sad. She pushed the emotion down, believing that such discouragement was sinful. She recited her joys: coming home to live with her beloved sister in the house their precious parents had built with such care. She thanked God for her family, her town, the church, the public library, the well-stocked stores, and so much more. She relaxed but couldn't get back to sleep. She got up and did her morning devotions, but something felt amiss. She laid down again and dozed.

At dawn, Arlene found herself standing in the eastern half of the house with its flow-through kitchen, dining room, and living room. Ma and Pa had designed this open space to fill with light, pouring in from the east through a series of large windows across the entire front. Today, the outer edges of the windows were icy—something Arlene had never seen anywhere on the African continent. Exterior flower boxes hung on the lower edge of each window, awaiting the arrival of spring. Inside, white valances framed the windows in typical Dutch fashion, and the curtains were drawn back.

Lights would soon blink on all over the neighborhood. Cars would pull out of driveways. Children would fill the schoolyard at the end of the block, marking the beginning of a new week. Arlene had unpacking ahead. She planned to find encouragement in the drawer full of "welcome home" mail. She knew the doorbell would ring many times. Grada had probably taken the day off from the grain elevator.

For the moment, however, all was still and quiet in the morning radiance. Arlene began to pray aloud in a language from afar. Was it Nuer? Amharic? Tonga? Tongues? Her prayer turned to song:

> When the trumpet of the Lord shall sound,
> And time shall be no more,
> And the morning breaks, eternal, bright, and fair . . .

She liked to sing this song at the start of the day, acknowledging that each morning was a promise, a foreshadowing of the dawn when she would meet Pa and they would sing this, his favorite hymn, together.

As the neighborhood slowly came to life, Arlene heard Grada in the other room. She returned to her bedroom to get ready for the busy day ahead. She dressed for bitter weather. Back in Zambia, she would have worn short sleeves. Here in Iowa, the harsh weather hinted at the culture shock she would soon experience, as she had so many times before. It was an almost comical transition. Sometimes after buying a car at Mouw's, she would turn out of the lot onto the left side of the highway, suddenly catching herself when she realized she no longer lived in a country with British traffic rules. Once she got a garage door opener installed. Searching for the light switch one morning, she hit the door opener by mistake, scrambling across the garage still in her nightgown. When she went shopping for clothes, she felt overwhelmed and even depressed with the racks and racks of options. Which style was appropriate, and why did it matter? Getting a malaria prescription filled at the local pharmacy always reminded her that she was from elsewhere, a place where malaria was as common as a cold.

She always spent the first few days seeing her hometown with fresh eyes. Almost everything was in contrast to where she used to live. The Hy-Vee grocery store parking lot was huge, paved, and completely without potholes. Lines were painted for parking spaces. When dusk fell, streetlights kept everyone safe getting to and from their cars. Almost everyone drove here; whereas in Zambia, pedestrians always outnumbered drivers.

The details of grocery shopping were especially striking. In front of the grocery store, bundles of wood and bags of softener salt rested in piles with no concern for thievery. The doors automatically slid open to welcome Arlene with a blanket of warm air to impede the wintery outside. Music played. The aisles were wide, the lighting was bright, and no shelf was empty. Here was everything a household needed for sustenance and personal maintenance. The apple choices alone included Braeburn, Cortland, both Red and Golden Delicious, Granny Smith, Macintosh, Gala, Jonathan, Fuji, and more. Workers kept every shelf tidy and all the floors clean.

Although Arlene appreciated the cleanliness, the overabundance of products nearly overwhelmed her. She told herself that the amount of goods really was a good thing. But if she could have Africa back, she would accept it on its own terms in a heartbeat.

To see Arlene at the Hy-Vee store was to see a tall, calm, white woman, very much resembling an Iowan. But the large hands that curled around the handle of her grocery cart were hanging on to an unseen world: a sky, a landscape, wild foliage, snakes, termite mounds, monkeys, crocodiles, hippos, drums, dances, languages, so many shades of black, histories thousands of years gone, the grass huts of southern Sudan, the modern reconstruction of Addis Ababa, the red bricks of rural Zambia—a myriad of religions, miracles, mysteries, stories, and stories upon stories.

This time, Arlene had brought that other world home with her, not only in her memory but also in diaries, letters, and photographs. She had boxes full—ink on paper, journals in stacks, letters on airform, slides in trays. There, in her tiny cursive, written throughout the heart of the twentieth century, was the demise of colonialism, the reformation of Christian missions, and Africa's embrace of modern medicine. In her photos and pages, as personal as her own breath, there was doubt and faith, despair and hope, loneliness and love.

She needed a new calling for this phase of her life. Her old call had been left behind on the other side of the world.

March had come in like a lion, but soon the snow turned to rain, tractors smoothed the gently rolling fields, and corn and beans began to sprout in long, perfect rows. Arlene wrote in her journal, *Beautiful Iowa*. Her calendar quickly filled with churches wanting her to speak, and her Sundays were scheduled solid for the coming year. She prepared several short talks accompanied by slides. She was delighted to meet people who had prayed daily for her for decades. But how would her life be sustained as those prayers faded? She needed those prayers even now. She was used to work and pressure—but it had been the classroom, the operating room, the bedside of a patient, and the mud floor in the hut of a dying man. The stresses of speaking tour were different and fatigued her terribly.

Arlene had much in common with other retired persons who awaken without their usual patterns and places. Unlike the average retiree, however, she had been taken out not only of her work, but also her house, her country, and away from friends and fellow worshipers. Many current Sioux Center residents had no idea who she was or what she had done.

Arlene had lived with bullets, power outages, mud, blood, and the desperate need for her medical services. Now she was in the United States—the place of the smooth road, the concrete sidewalk, the quiet inside of a car, the friendly police, the stocked shelves, dependable electricity, trimmed grass, and short waiting lines. There was little need for adrenaline here.

Slowly the depression came creeping in, and this time it seemed deeper than ever.

The ancient church might have called it *acedia*. In the thirteenth century, Thomas Aquinas described acedia as "the sorrow of the world." This did not refer to empathy, which would be sorrow *for* the world. Acedia referred to a burdensome sadness that resulted in a "why care" attitude. Throughout history, stories have been told of godly persons who, after a great endeavor, succumbed to soul-wrenching apathy. Think of Elijah after the victory over the prophets of Baal, sitting in the wilderness under the broom tree, asking God to end his life. Such an attitude can have a variety of causes. The pressures now on Arlene included too many choices and too few activities to which she could provide a meaningful contribution. Could a normally positive person succumb to great cynicism when faced with a sudden change of life? Who was Arlene to be beyond such danger?

Private worship, however, kept Arlene afloat. Her best friend, Vandy, counseled her, "It takes time on our faces before God, going through the crisis with him. We don't get faith by osmosis." So, Arlene lengthened her long-established pattern of daily intimacy with God, rising before 5:00 each day to begin her devotions.

But personal piety was not going to solve Arlene's problems. Her condition was not faithlessness. It was likely an undiagnosed mental disorder brought about by change and stress. Arlene received a letter from Macha with the report that Zambian money had devalued to seventeen kwacha per U.S. dollar. There was rioting in the Copperbelt. Her people were in duress, and here she was feeling helpless a world away. Her question "What can I do?" slid naturally to the despairing question, "What did I actually accomplish while I was there?" She was in that weakened state when a beloved friend made an unintentionally hurtful suggestion that financial support of missionary salaries was not a wise investment. It was better, he posited, to just send Bibles. That day Arlene wrote in her diary,

Sometimes I feel, Lord, like I failed you.

But true to her upbringing, she stuffed her emotions into the caverns of her subconscious. She carted her boxes of old diaries up to the attic and stowed her life story away.

Arlene was caught in a complex personal conundrum. In spite of her great compassion as a nurse, when it came to her own emotions, Arlene applied her generation's approach to pain: no coddling. Acknowledging pain, whether physical or emotional, was akin to complaining, which was a sign of immaturity in Arlene's book. She would have none of it. Complaints were tolerable if you were hospitalized, but the goal was to get beyond it all as quickly as possible. One could expect life to be painful, and grown-ups lived with the pain or at least hid it. She embraced the biblical maxim, "Consider it pure joy whenever you face trials." Take up your cross. Be like Christ.

Though few people knew it, Arlene continued to suffer from regular headaches. She wondered if the headaches indicated a resurgence of malaria, the disease she had contracted ten times during the past year alone. It impacted her sleep. One night she dreamed of the green blanket her neighbors had given her as a gift when she graduated from nursing school. Awakening with a start, Arlene remembered that she had lost that green blanket in Ethiopia. As she lay in the dark, she felt as if the blanket represented her: lost.

Arlene's outlook remained the same into midsummer. On July 19, United Flight 232 crashed fifty-three miles south of Sioux Center, resulting in the deaths of 112 souls on board. Arlene, Grada, and most of the region stayed glued to their televisions that week. Then at the end of the week, a family from Arlene's support group at church, the Bruxvoorts, lost their firstborn child in childbirth.

July 23 was the anniversary of Arlene's mother's death. Her devotions that morning brought her to Psalms 91 and 92.

With long life I will satisfy them,
  and show them my salvation. (Psalm 91:16)

In old age they still produce fruit;
  they are always green and full of sap. (Psalm 92:14) [NRSV]

She remembered a passage from Job, the book of sorrows, and wrote it alongside the other Scriptures she read that day:

You shall live a long, good life; like standing grain,
  you'll not be harvested until it's time. (Job 5:26) [TLB]

What did these verses mean to Arlene? Did they promise her long life? She, of all people, knew that tragedy filled the world, evidence that flew in the face of the promise of old age. As a medical professional, she had seen much youthful death. Jesus himself and many of his followers had died in their youth.

Arlene wrote in her journal that she needed those verses. Why? What did those verses mean to her as she arrived at the length of days they described? She was a farmer's daughter. She knew what a field of standing grain looked like. Did the image represent a reason to keep standing in hopes of a good harvest? Did the verses hold the prospect for productive, fruitful days ahead?

Arlene saw something else in those verses. She saw danger, a temptation she recognized from her earliest years on the mission field. She recognized her own perfectionism that made her work longer hours than were healthy for body, mind, or spirit. That made her feel personally responsible for the salvation of the lost. That made her desire to prove her worth through productivity.

Then she saw hidden in the verses a simple key that set her free from her most prudent self. The key was God, who would satisfy and save. This God would cause the fresh, green fruit to grow, and he would decide the time for the harvest.

Although her seeing God in the verses did not diminish her sense of personal responsibility, her joy was restored as she remembered she was not alone. She found relief in the truth that there were some things over which she had no control. That fall, Arlene copied into her journal a line from Oswald Chambers:

> *God puts his saints where they will glorify him,*
> *and we are no judges at all of where that will be.*

Her Africa chapters were closed. She had gained Iowa. She must find her heart's home here now.

What she did not yet know was that there was another potential cause of the headaches she had been experiencing. Before long she would be in a bed at the Mayo Clinic Hospital in Rochester, Minnesota, lying perfectly still, near death.

21

Headache

Bulwazi bulabila bukkazika moyo.
A patient who eats gives people hope of survival.

Awake at 5:00. My 70th birthday. "Make me to know thy ways, O Lord; teach me thy paths. Lead me in thy truth, and teach me, for thou art the God of my salvation; for thee I wait all the day long" (Psalm 25:4–5). "It is the Lord of the universe who calls you and offers you a place in his program. Sit in silence and wonder and expectancy" (Elisabeth Elliot). To Hardees for breakfast with Harriet. Ron Schaap came to open the driveway at 1:00 p.m. Dottie called about an uprising in Chiapas. Snowing again at night.

January 3, 1994

Arlene had experienced headaches for years. She assumed they were the result of malaria or malaria medications. She may have been correct. But the day after her seventieth birthday, a new sensation arose.

On that January Tuesday, she prepared an early lunch for five of her friends: egg casserole, sour cream coffee cake, and apple torte. Her friends left at noon, and after she washed up the dishes, she felt weary. This tiredness was not surprising since she had got up that morning at 3:00 a.m. Whenever she awoke in the wee hours, she always assumed it was God who woke her. She had a personal discipline of using the extra time of wakefulness for prayer and worship, rather than immediately trying to return to sleep.

So that afternoon, she took to her easy chair and dozed. After supper, she dozed some more, until little spastic pains woke her by stinging the left side and back of her head. Her legs also throbbed. She decided to go to bed and slept well until 5:30 the following morning. In the morning, the aches and pains were gone, and she let any concerns go.

Throughout that winter and summer, the old headaches occasionally returned for a day, but nothing more bothersome than what she had been experiencing for years. On the last Wednesday in August, however, she heard a swishing inside her head behind her left ear, along with a throbbing that was somewhat stronger than what she had felt in January. The symptoms ebbed and flowed during the following days. While the sensations were not severe, her medical-professional-self knew she was not well. After a week and a half, she telephoned her doctor.

"It's a throbbing behind my left ear. And sometimes I hear a swishing sound, but inside my head."

"Oh."

"Should I come in?"

"Have you taken an anti-inflammatory? Ibuprofen?"

"No."

"Start there and see how it responds. If you get a fever, come in."

She took the drug, and the throbbing remained—not a debilitation, but an annoyance. She gave the issue a bit more time. The symptoms were up and down, almost disappearing, then waking her up in the night. She prayed, of course, but she finally made an appointment to see her doctor. He cleaned a bit of wax from her ear and suggested she might have sinusitis. He gave her some sample decongestant tablets from his office supply drawer. Neither Arlene nor her doctor were overly concerned. The decongestant tablets made her sleepy, but she took them until they ran out.

On Tuesday, September 20, Arlene went to bed early with another headache. She was able to sleep, but the headache was worse when she awoke. It was beyond an ache—it was a pain on the left side. There was more. Her eyes weren't focusing and she couldn't read. She called the doctor's office, and he suggested they try a two-week course of antibiotics. Grada picked up the prescription from the pharmacist. The next day, Arlene felt somewhat better, so she assumed that an infection of some sort would be defeated in short order.

Arlene did feel better while taking the antibiotics; truth be told, the throbbing behind her ear sometimes lessened, sometimes increased, but it was still pretty much continuous. She wondered what was causing this drumbeat in her head and when the mystery would be solved.

On Monday, October 17, she was talking with her sister Bernice on the phone when the throbbing suddenly became strong. In that moment, she couldn't remember what she was trying to say to her sister. She made an excuse to end the conversation and called the doctor's office for an appointment. Nothing was available until three days later.

When her doctor saw her, his examination found nothing medically out of the ordinary. He ordered an MRI, and after she reclined motionless for forty-five minutes inside the sleeve of the large machine, no problem was revealed. So, her doctor prescribed Relafen, a stronger anti-inflammatory medication.

The throbbing lessened . . . then grew strong again. The doctor ordered a nasal smear. Negative. Arlene felt good one day and terrible the next. As autumn's color faded and the cold winds of November blew, northwest Iowa's farmers brought their harvest in from the fields. It was a time of gratitude and joy for the region, but the throbbing and swishing in Arlene's head didn't go away: the discomfort had become a constant presence in her life.

After the negative nasal smear, her doctor sought outside help. The first step he suggested was for her to return to the otolaryngologist who had done her sinus surgery nearly fourteen years earlier. At the end of the week, Grada and Arlene made the hour-and-a-half trek to Sioux Falls. Based on the synchronicity between the throbbing sensation and her own heartbeat, the specialist quickly narrowed this throbbing to a circulatory or blood vessel issue. He suggested that the MRI would not have detected an occlusion (blockage) in small vessels. Finally, he noted that her inability to focus and memory loss could be separate matters from the swishing sound and throbbing. She might have multiple conditions, but he couldn't be certain what those conditions might be.

The following day, former president of the United States Ronald Reagan released a letter to the nation sharing that he had been diagnosed with Alzheimer's. He wrote, "I now begin the journey that will lead me into the sunset of my life." Arlene could not help but wonder whether she, too, was approaching sunset.

Two days later, at 8:00 a.m., her vision blurred as it had back in September. Arlene called her doctor to report on her trip to Sioux Falls, as well as that morning's episode. She suggested going to Mayo Clinic in Rochester, Minnesota. Dr. Byer, who had introduced her to Macha, was on staff there. She could stay with him and his wife, Jeannie, while awaiting treatment. Her doctor noted that Mayo was a four-hour drive while Sioux City was only an hour. He said he would make an appointment at the closer hospital, and Arlene did not contradict him.

When Arlene told her sisters she was waiting for a call from the Sioux City hospital, each of them said, "Why not go to Mayo? Dave and Jeannie are there." That settled it. Arlene cancelled Sioux

City, and two days later she and Grada were on the way to register at Mayo as a "patient without an appointment." After putting her name on the list, they stayed the night with Dave and Jeannie. Arlene fasted just in case the hospital admitted her for blood work in the morning.

She was up at 5:45 a.m. and headed over to the clinic to wait on standby. She waited only until 10:00 a.m., which seemed quite good for a patient without an appointment. Was this due to prayer, or Dave's influence, or both? She never knew, but she received the medical care as a gift and gladly submitted to every sort of test under the sun. The doctors ran her through Alzheimer's assessments. She certainly had considered that diagnosis, along with the array of other possibilities any medical professional could imagine. The doctors learned she had come into close contact with HIV/AIDS in Macha, and that fact was entered into her chart.

By the end of her second day at Mayo, the doctors suspected Arlene had experienced one or more Transient Ischemic Attacks, or TIAs, caused when the blood supply was blocked to part of her brain. These were, in essence, mini-strokes, and the next one could be severe, even fatal. But what was the cause of the blockage? More tests were on the horizon.

Grada said goodbye and went home to Sioux Center for a couple of days, promising to be back soon. Arlene praised God for such a faithful sister.

The doctors first checked to see how well Arlene's heart was functioning. They put her to sleep for a transesophageal echocardiogram, placing a tube down her esophagus to take a close-up peek at her heart. She awakened with a sore throat and dry mouth and was glad when a nurse offered her some Jell-O and canned pears.

The next day was the angiogram, which was expected to reveal a great deal. A lengthy catheter would be extended through a blood vessel in her leg to carry dye into her brain, helping the radiologist to "map" her head. Arlene was awake for the procedure; and as a medical professional, she thought the whole process to be quite fantastic. A team of doctors (some in training) was present, and at one point the room fell silent. She knew what that meant: they had found something. Her imagination kicked in, and she wondered anew whether she would survive this yet unnamed affliction; and if she did, whether her senses might ultimately be impaired.

She was lying in her hospital bed when Dr. Cheng came to deliver the truth at last. She had a very rare condition known as an arterial venal fistula (also called "arteriovenous" or AVF). A fistula is an abnormal connection between body parts. In Arlene's case, a connection had grown between an artery and a vein in her brain, causing the blood to bypass certain capillaries and thereby deprive them of nutrients and oxygen.

The next day required a stress test to ensure she was strong enough for surgery. That was followed by a series, in the morning and again in the afternoon, of careful X-rays of her skull. By now, Grada had returned with the oldest Schuiteman sister Harriet. Those two slipped out for supper at 6:30, leaving Arlene alone when Dr. Cheng arrived to deliver her next report. She assured Arlene that she was strong enough for surgery and then showed her the X-rays. Abnormal veins and arteries spread over a large area. To someone like Arlene who was capable of understanding X-rays, the images were devastating.

The next steps, Dr. Cheng explained, would involve another team of doctors. On one day of surgery, they would embolize (obstruct) the abnormal blood vessels to control bleeding. Then in a subsequent procedure, they would eliminate the fistula radiologically with a gamma knife, or they might remove a section of her skull and do a surgical resection of the abnormal arteries that had previously been embolized.

"We, of course, hope," said Dr. Cheng, "that none of the potential side effects of these procedures will occur."

"What are they?" asked Arlene, knowing full well what the answer would be.

"Paralysis, loss of speech, blindness, deafness . . ."

"I understand," said Arlene. "And if we don't do the surgery?"

"Stroke. Sudden death."

"Right."

The following morning as Arlene did her devotions, she thanked God she could see the pages of her Bible, understand the words, and remember having read them before. She wrote in her journal that she was thankful she could write in her journal. Then she wrote,

> *Jesus, my times are in your hands. I want your will. Please let the remainder of my life be a fruitful one.*

One particular balm in this American Gilead was that she didn't need to drive an hour to find a phone. By reaching out her hand, she could touch the world—and during the long days of preparation and recuperation, the world could join Arlene in her room.

It was a journey back through her Africa career. She spoke with Dr. Bob Gordon, whom she had assisted with all those eye surgeries at the riverside clinic in Nasir, South Sudan. There was Dr. Roy Clark, who had received the fullness of the Holy Spirit before Arlene did at Mettu, Ethiopia. Then came Dr. John Spurrier, the surgeon from Macha, Zambia. So many other missionary friends called. She learned that Iteffa had stood on the platform at Mettu and invited her beloved church there to pray. Vandy called, several times. Endalcachow and his wife, Meseret, called, but they were not in the western mountains of Ethiopia. They were calling from North Carolina, of all places!

Arlene had always known Endalcachow to have a calm, deep spirituality. For this occasion, he chose a Bible passage specifically for her—Zechariah 4:7: "What are you, O mighty mountain? You will become level ground."

Arlene recognized a double meaning in this verse. Arlene herself had become leveled—immobilized, on her back, for hours. But there was more. She did not have the powers she once had. She no longer had a nameplate on an office door. She did not have the power to pass or fail a student. She did not drive cross-country to chair a committee that helped shape the medical future of a nation. She wrote in her journal:

> *When I hear of all who have called churches to pray, I feel humbled. Who am I, Lord? I am the recipient of Your tender care and love. I worship You. May Your great name be praised.*

Endalcachow's other message through this verse was that God had power over this medical condition. Fistula shmistula! God could level a mountain, or as Jesus once said, pick up a mountain and throw it into the sea. A fistula was easy for such a God. Arlene memorized Endalcachow's verse and recited it often during her Mayo days.

In spite of her faith, Arlene's emotions rose to the surface and her tears came in waves. During one of her many calls, her smart-alecky friend Vandy said, "Back in the eighties, I had a surgery right before Christmas, and they didn't expect me to live."

"What's your point?" said Arlene.

"Your surgery is right before Thanksgiving. Maybe holidays are a good sign."

"Sometimes you're silly, Vandy."

"Shall we pray about it?"

"Yes, we shall."

Grada was also helpful, not in a smart-alecky but a no-nonsense way. When Arlene got to listing all the possible side effects, Grada simply said, "We won't accept that."

On the day of the embolization, Arlene was in the surgical suite for six and a half hours. She was awake and watched the process on screens while lying perfectly still. That was the day the swishing sound stopped.

The next day, they shampooed her hair in preparation for shaving the left side of her head, and then the truth set in. She would be having a resection to finish the job. There were 47 surgical suites at this hospital with 140 operations each day. Her brain surgery would be one of those.

She slept peacefully until 3:30 a.m., then got out of bed and took a walk. Back in her room, she wrote in her journal:

Went for walk in hallways. Committed all my organs to God. His plan for me is fixed. He knows the outcome. It is well with my soul—not because of any righteousness of my own. Only because of the blood and righteousness of Jesus. Amazed at the peace which covers me and instills me. This is the day the Lord has made. I will rejoice and be glad in it. "What are you, O mighty mountain? You will become level ground."

They moved her into the operating room at 8:00 a.m., and she breathed in the general anesthetic for an all-day sleep. By 3:30, they brought word to her sisters that all had gone well and the bones were being wired back into place.

At 7:00 p.m., Arlene heard someone calling her name. It was Dr. Cheng. Arlene opened her eyes and saw Harriet, Grada, and Milly. She thought, "They're so beautiful. I can see them. I can talk. I can hear."

The day after a snowstorm, Arlene was discharged. Grada called the Minnesota State Patrol, who confirmed the interstate was cleared for travel. When the sisters pulled into Sioux Center that night, beloved friends had turned up the furnace, shoveled the drive, and laid supper on the table. Supper that night on Second Avenue was delicious.

The Sunday after Arlene returned from the Mayo Clinic happened to be her home church's first worship service in their new sanctuary. Arlene longed to be there. She had been the chair of one of the long-range planning subcommittees. As such, she had invested in the church's multiyear building project. Members of the congregation walked through Sioux Center that early Sunday morning. When they arrived at the church building, the cornerstone was revealed, the ribbon across the entry was cut, and the congregation filled the sanctuary to the ringing of bells and singing, "To God be the glory, great things he hath done."

Arlene knew she had no business being exposed to germs while she was on a healing journey. She made a decision and wrote in her journal,

Weather very foggy but mild. This is the day our church has looked forward to for so long. I am staying home.

22

Mountaintop

Meso aakabwenene taayindani lumwi.
Eyes that once saw each other will see
each other again.

---

*Met with Jeff and Jennifer in office at college. Working
on summer tour of "Iowa Ethiopia" and Jeff's next
priority is a fact-finding trip to Ethiopia. He wants
me to go along with him. This would be in October
followed by a trip with the whole drama team in
January, 2012 to perform "Iowa Ethiopia" according to
Matthew's invitation. I will have Dave communicate
directly with Jeff. Told Grada.*

April 19, 2011

Late in the evening of April 19, 2011, Dave Byer sent me (Jeff
Barker) an email. He introduced himself as a doctor who had worked
at Macha and had recommended Arlene as a nursing instructor there.
Dave had been following my series of plays about Arlene's career in
Africa, and he had learned from his Sioux Center sister that I was
planning to write a third play about her time in Zambia. Dave was
writing to say two things. First, he thought that it would be helpful if
I spent some time in Zambia. Second, he offered to pay for the trip.

I wrote back immediately to bring Dave up to speed with our
plans. Matthew Gichile, whom Arlene had met as a young man, was
now a university president in Addis Ababa. When he learned about
the play *Iowa Ethiopia*, he contacted me and urged me to bring the

Ethiopia story back to the place it had begun. My Northwestern College students and I wanted to say yes. None of us had yet been to the African continent, and I knew that performing in Ethiopia would be a life-changing experience for us all. I was eager to lead the cast there, but I felt as if I should go first to lay the groundwork for a performance tour. If Arlene felt strong enough for such a trip, then I wanted her to come along, even though she was eighty-seven at this point. I believed she was up to it.

During our spring break, she traveled with us on our cross-country tour of the play. Arlene was a great blessing to my students. After each performance, I introduced her and she would speak for only a minute, saying, "I want you to know that this is a true story. And that you, too, have a story that should be shared—the story of God at work in your life."

Once our van reached the East Coast, Arlene separated from us to visit her dear friend Vandy in Massachusetts. Vandy's house mate picked up Arlene following the performance of the play at the Warwick Center in New York and drove her back to Gloucester, so that the two old friends since Nasir days could visit in person. Vandy's heart was failing, and she rarely left her bed. But her mind was sharp and spirits joyful. She was ready, even eager, to be finished with her earthly struggle, for it was indeed a struggle now. The night before Arlene left, she wrote in her journal that they said,

"Our goodbye prayers of thanksgiving until we meet in heaven."

When I invited Arlene to return to Africa, she and I both knew what Grada's response was likely to be: "You cannot go unless I come along, and I am *not* coming along!" But as Arlene's Pa would have put it, "Arlene puts her mind to something, might as well get out of the way." Arlene waited and prayed, and her sisters eventually came around to her way of thinking.

Dave Byer's financial contribution gave us all hope, and my students raised additional funds throughout the summer months. Many people became our partners in the adventure. Two of our greatest partners were Arlene's key Macha medical colleagues, Phil Thuma and John Spurrier. These doctors had invested so much of their careers in the Macha mission. They now helped Arlene and me craft an itinerary and shepherded us through various medical and logistical travel challenges.

Arlene and I landed first in Ethiopia. At Addis Ababa airport, Arlene recognized someone at the luggage carousel. It was Pat Garamundi, who had been a Peace Corps worker with her husband, John, at Mettu. As Arlene approached her, she broke into a huge smile.

"I kept looking over, Arlene, to see if that was you!" She was now returning to show her daughter the place where she and John became Christians. John went on to became the lieutenant governor of California and in 2009 was elected to the U.S. House of Representatives.

One day while we were in Addis, Nyakota came to the guesthouse. She was not as old as Arlene, but she seemed much older. Nyakota was the one whose husband, Reet, was a lay preacher and dresser at the Nasir clinic. He had refused to follow the traditional practice of burning his wife's feet after their baby had died. Now here she stood embracing Arlene, singing and chattering in Nuer. Even after all this time, Arlene understood every word.

I got to meet Reverend Iteffa Gobena—the evangelist who, as a young man, counseled Arlene about speaking in tongues. He became the president of the Ethiopian Evangelical Church Mekane Yesus, the largest Lutheran denomination in Africa. We had dinner with Pastor Iteffa and the family of Matthew Gichile, who was now the president of New Generation University College.

One day, Arlene and I were standing in the Addis International Airport, waiting for a flight to the western mountains. A tall black man was standing with a group of white persons, and Arlene recognized him as Nuer by the markings on his forehead. She went over to him, said something in Nuer, and he smiled.

In Nuer, she said, "I am Nya BiGoaa Jon of Nasir."

I saw the man's eyes grow wide. "Nya BiGoaa? Nya BiGoaa!"

"Yes."

"Friends, come here!" he said in English as he waved the group of white people over. "This is Nya BiGoaa. She once lived in my home town. I've never met her, but I heard of her and Nyarial [Vandy] all my life. So many of us became Christians because of them. I never thought I would meet her."

Arlene asked, "What is your name?"

"I'm Michael Gat Kek. These people are from the church I pastor in Portland, Maine. We're on a mission trip. It's difficult to get to Nasir, so we're traveling to Gambela, and then we'll take a boat up river. No borders to cross."

"I wish I could go with you," said Arlene.

"I wish it too. Wait till I tell the people back home that I met Nya BiGoaa."

Once we got to the western mountains, Arlene and I worshiped in one of the churches where the great Ethiopian revival began. There we heard the pan-African sound of ululation and witnessed the elderly women playing drums. Pastor Yonas taught me that African worship is "jumping and dancing as much as singing—maybe even more so."

The Zambian part of our journey began with a flight into Lusaka. There we met up with a Johns Hopkins professor, Doug Norris, who was connected with the Macha Research Trust, the official name of the institute for studying malaria in the region. He told us that the pilot of the four-seater Cessna that would fly us to the Macha air-field was still fueling the plane and doing paperwork. As we waited, Doug gave me a wonderful introduction to the local culture. "You're about to meet some of the happiest people in the world. You go out to the villages, and all the children are happy. They have *nothing*, yet they're happy." He made a grimace. "Western culture. We think we get happiness by collecting things."

I asked Doug what he had learned about malaria here, and he answered, "It's a myth that malaria mosquitos feed late at night. We used to think that if you covered yourself with a mosquito net when you went to bed, you were safe. But mosquitos are adaptable. Once they learn that everyone is covered up with nets by 10:00 p.m., they start feeding at 8 p.m."

Arlene was thrilled to climb into the Cessna. She had often flown out of Lusaka on large airplanes, but she had never before seen Macha from the air: the Macha airstrip was new. As soon as we landed, we met Phil Thuma who became our primary tour guide for our too few days at the mission.

It was dry season, so the only green growth we saw was a few fresh weeds and the perfectly manicured and irrigated gardens at the Macha Research Trust. We stayed in the residences, which were elegant in their simplicity, built with locally baked brick made from the waste of termite mounds. Each building had colorful stucco identity bands individually designed by Elaine Thuma and Esther Spurrier. Their husbands, the doctors Phil and John, were so much alike that some said they could finish each other's sentences. But we were told that Elaine and Esther were even closer; they were soulmates.

Phil guided us to the nursing school where we met Doreen Sitali, the current Zambian head tutor. She was the partial fulfill-ment of the Zambianization of the staff that Arlene, Phil, and John had worked toward thirty years earlier. Although Phil was almost a Macha native, his medical work was now on a voluntary basis a few days a week. He now spent most of his time researching malaria.

I noticed a black-and-white photograph hanging on the wall of Doreen's office, the same office that had once been Arlene's. I moved close to the photo to read the inscription that had been written at the bottom in black ink:

Marie Ann Traver from Wainfleet, Ontario, Canada served as a nurse at Macha Hospital – Zambia. She contracted cerebral malaria and went to be with her Lord in September of 1975.

The school now had twice as many students as when Arlene departed twenty-two years prior. Doreen took us to a classroom where we interrupted the lecture just long enough for Arlene to be introduced and say a few words. She said, "I'll tell you what I used to remind all my students. You have been given a great privilege in being chosen to sit here. There are hundreds of others waiting for your chair the moment you feel this work is too difficult for you to continue. I pray that you will be able to finish well."

Next, we visited the malaria research lab and also toured the TB and HIV/AIDS labs that were nearly completed. I received an education on mosquitos. Only a certain type of mosquito is equipped to carry the malaria parasite. Mosquitos bite from smell. They will not bite a bag of blood, but the smell of dirty clothes will lead a mosquito back to the same hut they visited before. I learned how these facts were discovered. Phil's team had found a way to dye the mosquitos for study during the insect's one-to-three-month life span! That day we got to see the pans of *Anopheles* larvae swimming like little fish waiting to burst into flight within twelve hours.

After lunch at the school cafeteria, we drove to Choma on the new asphalt road laid just a couple of years before. We were on a mission to locate the Shamapani family near Choma. Enoch Shamapani had been the much-beloved pastor at Macha while Arlene lived and worked there. Later he became a bishop of the Brethren in Christ Church of Zambia. Phil did not know exactly where the family's new house was, so he kept slowing down his truck to ask people. Phil told us that he never lets Zambians know he's coming. If he does, they'll have killed a chicken and prepared a meal.

We soon found the Shamapanis. They invited us in, and the old friends caught up with one another. I learned that Enoch had helped to write the new constitution for the country of Zambia. He said, "That's how I bought the bricks to build this house. The new constitution paid for them!" We spent an hour with Enoch, his wife Lastina, their son Eric, and their two-year-old grandson. Enoch reminded us that Zambians have much in common with Hebrew culture: "When Jesus said, 'A sower went out to sow,' we understand that. We still sow here. All these fields around were sown by hand."

Before leaving Choma, Phil filled his truck with petrol (at a price equivalent to $8 a gallon). During the hour drive back, Phil paused to point out where the truck ran Arlene off the road. The location was not easy to spot because the sharp curve had been lengthened when they paved the road. Arlene said it was holy ground.

That night we dined at the local restaurant, but it wasn't the sort of restaurant with a menu. Phil and John had sent a message that morning that we were coming, and the restaurant chose our meal. A few other friends joined us. Elaine and Esther were stateside and would meet us in Pennsylvania.

We had a long, leisurely conversation somewhat about old times, but more so about developments in both malaria and AIDS research.

"When I sit in church and see the children," Phil said, "I know that we've made progress. "We have a model that has all but eradicated malaria. Malaria is down in the Macha catchment by 98 percent."

"How did you do it?" I asked.

"It's a combination of factors, but it's built on the principal of test and treat."

"Meaning what?"

"It's similar to the lesson of Typhoid Mary. Typhoid Mary didn't get sick from typhoid, but she also didn't wash her hands. So, the typhoid was passed out of her. She was an asymptomatic carrier of the disease, and she helped spread the plague because she wasn't tested or treated. Adults in this region who have contracted malaria enough times might be asymptomatic but still a conduit for the disease. A mosquito might not be carrying the parasite when it enters a hut. But it could bite an infected adult, pick up the parasite, then bite a child for whom the disease could be deadly. Malaria Mary. That's why it's so important we test everyone, even those who don't think they're sick."

John chimed in. "And it's the same with HIV/AIDS. AIDS can be controlled with 'test and treat.' But there's the stigma of being tested, so we have this motto: Everyone is positive until tested negative."

John continued to share about significant advancements in HIV/AIDS therapies. As Phil had been called to work on malaria, John's calling in recent years had leaned toward HIV/AIDS care. I was stunned to learn that since 2004, Macha's antiretroviral medication program had developed to the extent that the Macha team was seeing HIV positive mothers able to bear children with no evidence of the disease. I was also surprised to hear that AIDS prevention was discussed at every church business meeting. I could not remember being present at a church meeting in the United States in which a compassionate response to any disease was on the agenda, let alone a sexually transmitted disease.

The highlight of the night was when John told us about God's calling on the lives of two young American couples. None of these individuals were medical professionals, but they felt responsible to serve those affected by HIV/AIDS.

John grimaced and smiled at the same time as he said, "Esther and I spoke with these couples. Each of them felt called to come to Macha. They met each other after hearing us speak, and they all felt the same calling. Given the lack of support from their parents, I wonder if I should feel guilty. The one father won't even discuss the possibility. But it's now a year later, and their callings have not faded. They want to come. We just don't yet know how they will be supported." It struck me that the question was no longer "Who will go?" but instead "Who will you support?" Arlene's church had answered that second question and together with Arlene they had lived a mission, a calling, a story.

The restaurant lights flickered and then went out. The generator was done for the day, so we sat for a while in the candlelight. Then Arlene began to pray, and the veil between heaven and earth grew thin.

During our last day in Macha, we rested in the afternoon before riding with Phil to the home of Abraham and Vera. Vera was Arlene's former student and now a nurse, and Abraham was the chief administrator of the hospital. They had invited many old friends and acquaintances of Arlene's. As we arrived, nurses who had once called Arlene teacher poured out of the house wearing their brightly flowered *chitenges*, clapping their hands, and singing a Tonga song. Arlene stood by Phil's truck and beamed as they rushed forward to embrace her.

Once we all crowded into the living room, the evening officially began with prayer by a Dutch man who was now living in Macha. He had started some local businesses—the airstrip, the wireless network, and the restaurant where we had eaten. His demeanor was strong almost to the point of harsh, especially when set against the tapestry of Zambian demureness. His wonderful prayer, however, affirmed that the kingdom of God was among us. He thanked God for the people on whose shoulders we stood, and how some of those shoulders were present there that night. He affirmed that we all have a great commission, and that we are all the head, not the tail—more than conquerors in Christ Jesus, in whose name he blessed our evening together.

Several people spoke—starting with the elders, followed by younger voices. Then, before we ate from the buffet that had been laid out (two kinds of cabbage, rice, a mashed-potato-like food you roll in your hands, varieties of chicken and pork, beans, and cake), a woman knelt and washed Arlene's hands. Other women stooped in front of the men and poured water on our hands to cleanse them. Phil whispered to me that it was traditional for Zambian women to bring water to pour over the hands of the men of the household. After this traditional washing was complete, Arlene was directed to the food first, followed by the men, and then the women.

During the meal, two more of Arlene's previous students arrived. They had learned about this event the previous day. The two had made their way to Choma and caught a ride in a minivan toward Macha. The van kept breaking down, so they somehow got word to Abraham, who sent a driver to get them. They didn't even know where they would sleep that night; but they were there, arriving late, offering speeches of gratitude, and then sitting at Arlene's feet for the remainder of the evening.

The final speech of the night was given by an ex-nursing student of Arlene who knelt as she began to speak. She said something in Tonga, and Phil whispered to me that she had, "I am not worthy to stand."

Arlene and I had scheduled our journey to end at an annual event in eastern Pennsylvania called "Zambash," held at the Spurrier's stateside residence in the heart of Brethren in Christ country. I expected a casual gathering for reminiscing among fellow Americans who had once lived and worked in Zambia. How wrong I was! The event was for stoking the fire of enduring vision and continuing endeavor. These were passionate Christians participating in a mission they knew couldn't be accomplished within their lifetimes. Still, they met annually to check and prod and hope and pray and encourage and scheme and believe that the work of the Lord Jesus Christ would continue in and through Zambia.

Vandy expected her heart would stop before we returned from Africa, but she was to suffer four more years until she was eighty-nine and Arlene was ninety-one. Vandy spent most of those years in bed. The two former missionary colleagues spoke often, until Vandy was too weak to have more than one or two conversations a day with anyone. Then Arlene second-guessed every call, not wanting to over-tax her friend or steal her away from other needful conversations.

When Vandy asked Arlene "How you are?" if Arlene said, "Not feeling too well today," Vandy would chide her, "If you get to the top of the mountain before me, it won't sit too well!"

On one of their final phone calls, Vandy said, "I've decided on the epitaph for my tombstone."

"Are you sharing, or do you want it to be a surprise?"

"*Nyarial ε ram anath.*"

"A person of the people."

"I guess you had a good tutor in Nuer."

"I had the best tutor," Arlene said, referring to Vandy.

"I've got to go now, Arlene," Vandy said. "But I'll be looking for you when you come."

On the evening of October 26, 2015, Arlene received the news that Vandy had finally reached the mountaintop. Arlene journaled,

This is wonderful for her. I slept fitfully. I knew this day was coming but now it is sinking in. So many scenarios came into my mind in the night. Vandy seeing Jesus face to face! How she used to sing that song in the Sudan:

> *Face to face, O blissful moment!*
> *Face to face—to see and know.*

Face to face with my redeemer,
Jesus Christ who loves me so.

Vandy slipping out of her decaying, wasted body with joy. Seeing the familiar faces after being spellbound by Jesus. Maybe she is still in that spellbound position now! The Light, the Joy, the Beauty.

Arlene called me the night Vandy died. I put the word out to the dozens of students and colleagues who had worked on the plays. The next day, Arlene came to my office to work on the first book in this trilogy, *Sioux Center Sudan*. I told her I was planning to attend Vandy's memorial service, and I asked her if I could make arrangements for us to travel together. Our office manager, Jennifer, was willing to accompany Arlene. After much consideration, Arlene agreed.

Vandy's memorial service was held in a classic colonial-style New England congregational church on the rocky Eastern seaboard in Lanesville, Massachusetts. After the service, we gathered in the parish hall to share memories. Arlene commented on Vandy's sense of humor, beautiful singing voice, and the keen mind that helped her unravel the intricacies of the Nuer language.

A woman I didn't know stood up and said, "Everyone felt as if they were the one Van loved best. She had that way with people. But I really was the one she loved best."

There was laughter in the room. I immediately understood the woman's comment. Vandy had made me feel like an old friend the very first time I heard her voice—when she sang to me in Nuer over the phone so I could hear the sounds of that language. But I knew I was not her best friend. Everyone there knew the same. Even Arlene, who was close to being her best friend, knew that neither she nor Vandy trafficked in such earthly competitions. The True Friend for both of them was far and away greater and more permanent and more real.

Selected Bibliography

Baillie, John. *A Diary of Private Prayer*. New York: Charles Scribner's Sons, 1949.

Barker, Jeff, *Arlene: An African Trilogy*. Play presented by Northwestern College Theatre Department, Orange City, Iowa, 2014.

———. *Iowa Ethiopia*. Play presented by Northwestern College Theatre Department in the United States and Ethiopia, 2011–12 and 2019.

———. *Iowa Ethiopia: A Missionary Nurse's Journey Continues*. Peabody, MA: Hendrickson, 2019.

———. *Sioux Center Sudan*. Play presented by Northwestern College Theatre Department in North America and Japan, 2006–10.

———. *Sioux Center Sudan: A Missionary Nurse's Journey*. Peabody, MA: Hendrickson, 2018.

———. *The Storytelling Church: Adventures in Reclaiming the Role of Story in Worship*. Cleveland, TN: Webber Institute Books, 2011.

———. *Zambia Home*. Play presented by Northwestern College Theatre Department on tour in North America, 2013.

Davidson, Hannah Frances. *South and Central Africa: A Record of Fifteen Years' Missionary Labors*. Elgin, IL: Brethren Publishing House, 1915.

Faithful, George. "The Evangelical Sisterhood of Mary: Profile of a Protestant Monastic Order." Collected Faculty and Staff Scholarship (2009), 313. https://scholar.dominican.edu/all-faculty/313.

Froemke, Heidi. "Greetings from Zambia." *Frontier Nursing Service Quarterly Bulletin* 63, no. 2 (1987): 19–22.

Hammarskjöld, Dag. *Markings*. Translated by Leif Sjöberg and W. H. Auden. New York: Alfred A. Knopf, 1975.

Hurnard, Hannah. *Mountains of Spices*. Living Books, 1983.

Kimmel, Carolyn. *First a Friend: The Life and Legacy of Alvan and Ardys Thuma*. CreateSpace, 2015.

Lapp, John. *Anabaptist Songs in African Hearts: A Global Mennonite History*. Intercourse, PA: Good Books, 2006.

McClure, William Donald. *Red-Headed, Rash, and Religious: The Story of a Pioneer Missionary*. Board of Christian Education of the United Presbyterian Church of North America, 1954.

Mumpande, Isaac. *Tonga Proverbs*. Harare: Silviera House, 2001.

Partee, Charles. *Adventure in Africa: The Story of Don McClure*. Grand Rapids: Zondervan, 1990.

Preston, Richard. *The Hot Zone: A Terrifying True Story*. New York: Anchor Books, 1995.

Ratmeyer, Una. *Hands, Hearts, and Voices: Women Who Followed God's Call*. New York: Reformed Church, 1995.

Schlink, M. Basilea. *Repentance: The Joy-Filled Life*. Minneapolis: Bethany House, 1984.

Stackhouse, John G., Jr. *Can God Be Trusted: Faith and the Challenge of Evil*. New York: Oxford University Press, 1998.

Swart, Morrell F. *The Call of Africa: The Reformed Church in America Mission in the Sub-Sahara, 1948–1998*. Historical Series of the Reformed Church in America. Grand Rapids: Eerdmans, 1998.

Vandevort, Eleanor. *A Leopard Tamed*. Fiftieth anniversary issue, with new foreword and introduction. Peabody, MA: Hendrickson, 2018. First published 1968 by Harper and Row.

Arlene's view out of the plane on her first flight into Lusaka, the capital city. After Zambia's independence in 1964, city life became vastly different for the indigenous population (1978).

Josh, the dog that came with the blue Datsun (1979).

The oxcart was a valuable tool seen everywhere in the Zambian countryside (1979).

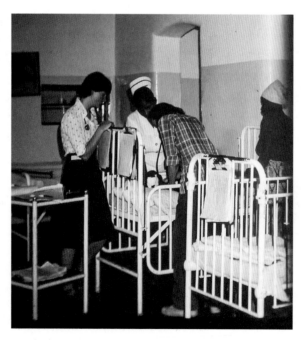

The pediatric ward at Katete, where the number of patients often required two to a crib (1980).

The Reformed Church of Zambia, where services were held in the Nyanja language (1980).

Glenn Bruggers was Arlene's Reformed Church in America mission supervisor. He is on the left with his wife, Phyllis, visiting with James and Faith Cairns at Katete (1980).

Set 56 at Katete Nurses Training School, where the student body became co-ed while Arlene was the principal tutor (1980).

Partison Zulu and Charles Mumba, soldiers from the nearby camp, came to witness for Christ at Katete (1979).

Matthew Gichele, a refugee of Ethiopia who knew many of Arlene's old friends, came to visit Arlene at Katete (1980).

Arlene's photo of *Mosi-oa-Tunya* ("The Smoke That Thunders") on the Zambezi River, the largest waterfall in the world, located near the town of Livingston at the intersection of Namibia, Botswana, and Zimbabwe. The English name for the falls is Victoria Falls, after the British queen, and the town is named after the Scottish doctor and explorer, David Livingstone (1980).

Arlene overlooking the stunning Malawi landscape along the southeastern border of Zambia (1980).

On holiday with the Cairns and Father Hewitt, Arlene watched the sun dance on Lake Malawi, the 360-mile-long sliver of water that extends along two-thirds of the eastern edge of Malawi from Tanzania to Mozambique (1980).

Marie Ann Traver
from Wainfleet, Ontario, Canada
served as a nurse at Macha
Hospital-Zambia from January
to September 1975. She contracted
cerebral malaria and went to be
with her Lord on September 11, 1975

Photo of Marie Ann Traver that still hangs on the wall of the Macha Nurses Training School.

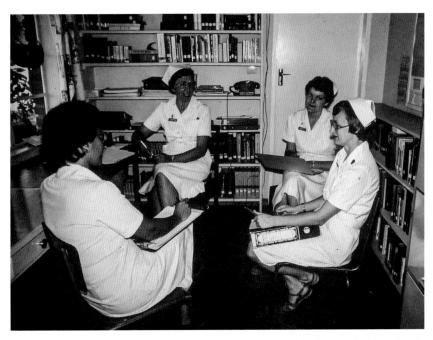

Arlene leading a meeting in her office with the Nurses Training School teaching staff at Macha (1982).

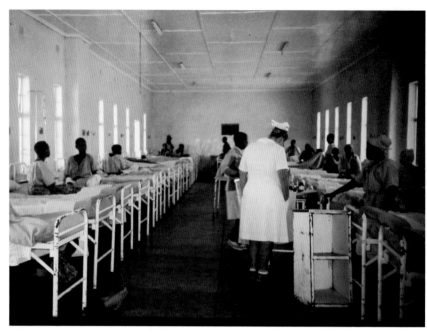

The women's ward at the Macha hospital. Narrow space between beds forces medical staff to squeeze through sideways (1985).

This mother's skin disease on her leg does not stop her from tending both her child and her crop (1982).

"The Fires" is the area where family members eat and sleep, sometimes for days at a time, while waiting for their loved one in the hospital (1982).

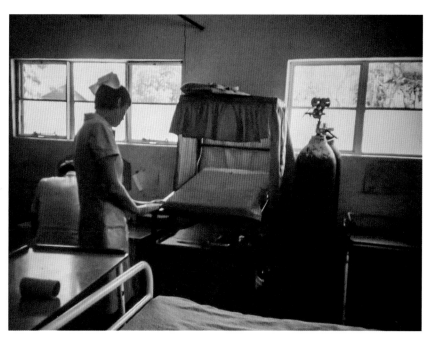

The incubator for premature babies (1986).

Macha Primary School. Notice three or even four children to a desk, the use of school uniforms, and no shoes. The boys sit on one side of the room and girls on the other. Segregation by gender is common at both school and church (1982).

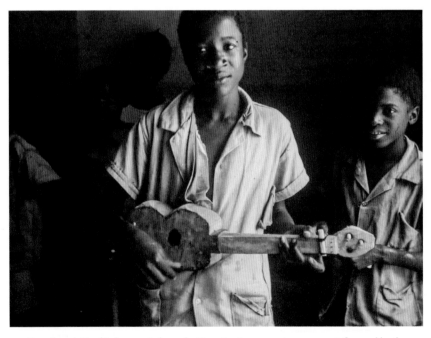

Even though Zambia became independent in 1964, its pop music scene was influenced by the rock and roll of Britain and America. This boy had no guitar, so he made his own (1982).

A local store, across from the primary school (1986).

A local medicine woman, whose dance was part of her therapies for sale (1986).

Arlene began parking her blue Datsun near her bedroom window
after its wheels were stolen one night (1984).

Doris, Arlene's office manager, with her husband and baby in
front of their traditional-style home (1988).

Fisher's Bridge on the Choma Road before it was paved, where Arlene's close call occurred (1988).

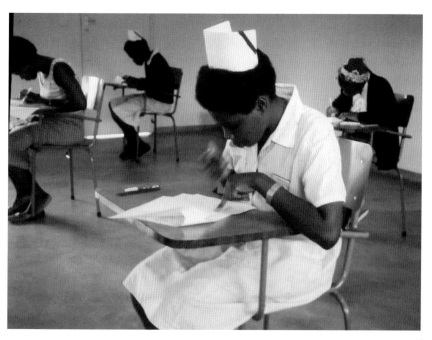

The final exam for Arlene's final class at Macha (1988).

Laundry at the Nurses Training School continues to be done outdoors. The clothesline includes blue-and-white nursing uniforms, along with the multipurpose traditional fabric swath *chitenge* (2011).

Eventually the Choma Road was paved, but travel habits remain. The road has many pedestrians and bicyclists, even out in the countryside, and vehicle breakdowns are dealt with directly on the roadway. Night driving remains especially dangerous (2011).

While AIDS education indicates modern Zambia, traditions continue with women transporting burdens on their heads and wearing *chitenge* to cover their legs (2011).

Dr. Phil Thuma in Macha (photo courtesy of David Colwell, JHSPH, 2011).

Esther and John Spurrier (photo courtesy of Dwight Rotz, 2017).

The Wayside Chapel north of Sioux Center, Iowa (photo taken 2020).

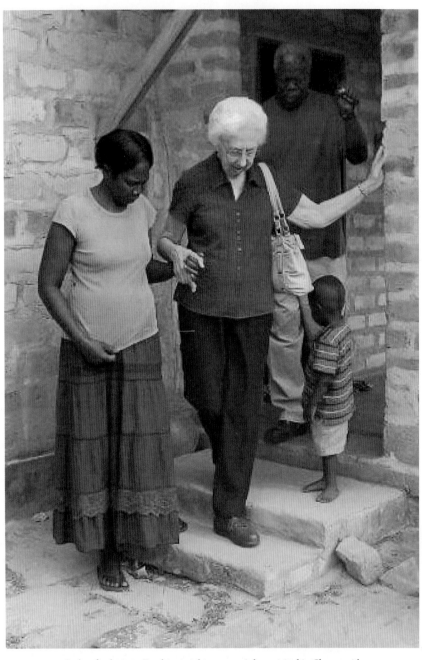

On her final trip to Zambia at eighty-seven, Arlene visited in Choma with
Bishop Enoch Shamapani, who had been her pastor at Macha (2011).